DIARY
of a TV Waitress

Renae The Waitress

Renae The Waitress

Photos throughout the book appear in courtesy of Phil Johnson, photographer and permission of Larry Black, Gabriel Communications

Copyright © 2014 by Renae The Waitress, LLC

All rights reserved. Except as permitted under the US Copyright Act of 1976 no part of this publication may be reproduced, distributed, or transmitted in any form or by any means, or stored in a database or retrieval system, without written permission of the publisher.

Renae The Waitress, LLC
Renae Johnson
PO Box 210796
Nashville TN 37221

Visit my website at www.Renaethewaitress.com or www.Larryscountrydiner.com

Printed in the USA, 2014

Acknowledgements

Dear Diner Guests,

    What you are about to read in these pages are some very personal, honest and maybe even some treasured secrets about becoming a TV waitress. It is not for the faint of heart or picky eaters. I will however, protect the innocent and sugar coat the facts. My story contains multiple twists and turns and will never cause folks to cry over spilt milk. I will share my tips with you but in the end remember, " The cameras are always rolling...and we don't care."

    Of course this book would not be possible without, the help & support of my DINER family (Larry, Keith, Jimmy, Michele and Nadine) and the following *Country Music Legends:*

Bill Anderson, James Gregory, The Whites, Charlie McCoy, John Conlee, T. Graham Brown, Gene Watson, Jeannie Seely, Jim Ed Brown, Bobby Bare, Larry Gatlin, Teea Goans, Ed Bruce, Gordon Mote, Ray Stevens, Sonny Curtis, Riders In The Sky, Ray Pillow, Gary Morris, The Grascals, Mandy Barnett, The Isaacs, George Hamilton IV, Ronny Robbins, Time Jumpers, Jan Howard, Billy Dean, Mike Snider, Shelly West, Dan Miller, Moe Bandy, Billy Grammar, Dallas Frazier, Johnny Counterfit, Joe + Rory, Buddy Greene, Jeff Taylor, Justin Trevino, Ralph Emery, Jimmy Fortune, Neal McCoy, Carl Jackson, Larry Cordle, Con Hunley, Barbara Fairchild, Susy Bogguss, Aaron Tippin, Dailey & Vincent, Doyle Lawson, The Roys, The Cleverlys, Rhonda Vincent, Jean Shepard, Robyn Young, Rodeo & Juliet, Buck Trent, Johnny Lee, Oak Ridge Boys, Exile, Jimmy C. Newman, Collin Raye, Leona Williams, David Frizzell, Linda Davis, Mac Wiseman, Janie Fricke, LuLu Roman, Quebe Sisters, Marty Raybon, Buddy Jewell, Daryl Singletary, The Bellamy Bros, Red Steagall, Mark Chestnut, Wilson Fairchild, Helen Cornelius, Joe Stampley, Steve Hall and Shotgun Red, Freddy Weller, Dickey Lee, John Berry, Georgette Jones, Baillie and The Boys, Jim Lauderdale, Eddy Raven, Guy Penrod, LaDonna Gatlin, Wilford Brimley, Mo Pitney, Williams and Ree, Charlie Daniels, The Texas Tenors, Sweethearts of the Rodeo, Roy Clark, Restless Heart, John Anderson, The Easters, Billy Yates, BJ Thomas, The Roys, Jim Glaser, Tracy Lawrence, Larry Mahan, Rebecca Lynn Howard, Ricky Skaggs, Mark Lowry, Jet Williams, Mark Wills, Bobby Osborne, Mickey Gilley, TG Sheppard, Gary Chapman, Carolyn Martin, Tony Orlando, Hot Club of Cowtown, Bill Medley, Jim Menzies, the Church Sisters, Col. Littleton, Johnny Rodriguez, Hoot Hester, Jarrett Dougherty, Jamie O'Neal.

Thank you — Renae the Waitress

Menu

★ 1 — The Perfect Recipe for a Successful Show ... 1

★ 2 — More Than a Waitress ... 11

★ 3 — Sassy Diner Attire ... 21

★ 4 — That's No Waitress ... 29

★ 5 — Squeaky Door ... 37

★ 6 — "This isn't Burger King" ... 43

★ 7 — The Counter ... 51

★ 8 — Got Pie? ... 61

Menu

- **9** Travelin' Waitress ... 69
- **10** Mind Your Manners ... 77
- **11** TV Diner Lingo ... 85
- **12** Ask Your Waitress ... 105
- **13** Reservations ... 113
- **14** Diner Stories ... 123
- **15** Paparazzi 101 ... 129
- **16** In Case of Emergency ... 131

The Perfect Recipe for a Successful Show

The first week Larry's Country Diner went on the air, everyone kind of scratched their heads. The concept of taking people who knew nothing about television and creating a show that folks would actually watch week after week was pretty crazy. But what was even crazier was that the cast, myself included, didn't even consider it. We had no script, no rehearsals, no coaching and *definitely* no experience. We didn't even know what we didn't know. But what we found out is that people are looking for something genuine – the real deal.

I had worked with Larry Black for more than eleven years, and I knew him well enough to know that this crazy idea of me being a TV waitress could work, and I wasn't gun-shy or paralyzed at the notion that I might fail. I had no advantage of perspective or hindsight. Inexperience enables you to get on the path and move. And move is what I did. I didn't do it the right way all the time, but I sure had fun trying.

I remember Larry saying, "Now, if you dig yourself in a hole, you are going to have to dig yourself out, 'cause we're not stopping tape." What in the world does that mean? How would I dig myself into a hole? How would I dig myself out? I figured it must be some kind of TV lingo that wouldn't apply to me. Boy, was that a blonde moment! It didn't take long for me to figure out that it most certainly included me. However, I also discovered that digging yourself out of a hole can be more fun than going around a hole.

People are looking for a road map to success. I guess my view is that success has to start with passion. And real passion can only come from something you really love. I am not sure I am a successful waitress in the eyes of the service industry, but I have passion for what I do. I make sure my inexperience doesn't feed arrogance, which would surely spell failure. I truly love hearing the theme song and walking through the swinging door onto the set of Larry's Country Diner. I am pretty sure on the other side of that door I will be surrounded by people I love, people who love me back. That may sound like a strange statement for waitress and most certainly for a television show waitress. Our show definitely doesn't fit the entertainment mold for a success. Or does it?

> "...you are going to have to dig yourself out, 'cause we're not stopping tape."

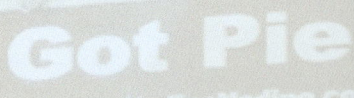

When you think back to some of the more successful television series, don't you wonder if Aunt Bee and Barney hung out together or if John-Boy Walton even liked Mary Ellen, Ben, Erin, Jim Bob, Jason or Elizabeth? How about the Fonz? Do you think he and Richie Cunningham spent vacations together?

We've had industry executives drop by Larry's Country Diner trying to analyze the chemistry of the diner show. I don't even know what that means, exactly. What I do know is that Jimmy, Keith, Larry, Nadine and I have friendships that began long before the Diner show and will continue long after it is off the air. We have gone on vacations together, attended the same church, celebrated birthdays, enjoyed dinner and movies together. We are all very good friends. Or should I say, family? I guess that is chemistry.

Friends.

Diner Lingo Quiz

What are "sinkers & suds" in diner lingo?
a. Cookies and milk
b. Doughnuts and coffee
c. Sugar cubes and tea
d. Peanuts and beer

Answer: Chap 11

TV Diner Jokes

Q: What do you call a pig thief?

A: A hamburglar.

Q: Where do they hold prizefights in Fastfoodland?

A: In an onion ring!

Q: Where are the best tacos served?

A: In the Gulp of Mexico!

Diner Lingo Quiz

What is" Italian perfume?
a. The spice rack
b. Sweet sausage
c. Garlic
d. Burnt sauce

Answer: Chap 11

More Than a Waitress

With respect to dreams or goals in life, television or waitressing were the two careers furthest from my mind. My only experience on TV came as a contestant on The Price is Right. I learned waitressing while a flight attendant for America West Airlines. But let me explain.

In 1991, I began work for America West in Phoenix, Arizona. Because of the Gulf War, it was a terrible time and the airline was struggling. Although I had been trained in reservations, gates, corporate security and the ramp, the airlines started laying employees off, with the promise of rehire in time. My family and I had just moved from Nashville to Arizona, so this was unexpected.

One day I got a phone call from a group of girls, fellow airline employees, who were planning a trip to Burbank, California to attend The Price is Right. It was a 100-minute flight, and we planned to set out in the morning and return home that evening. This sort of daytrip was not unusual. Working for the airlines comes with flight benefits. My girlfriends needed a certain number of airline employees to get tickets to the show. My best friend was going, and counting on me to go, too. Even though I was not a big fan of the show, the daytrip with the girls sounded fun. We boarded our flight at Sky Harbor Airport early the next morning and touched down at Burbank Airport in plenty of time.

Outside NBC studios, we joined the rather long line that had already formed. There was an air of excitement as more and more folks joined the line. I could hear them talking about being a contestant on the show and the various games, the wheel and the final showcase. I knew immediately I was out of my league. The only thing I knew about the show was that the host was Bob Barker and that you had to guess prices of stuff. Stuff, I had no clue about. At some point, while slowly moving up in line, we were handed forms and asked to fill in our name, address and social security number. I learned this was standard procedure since several lucky folks would win prizes and money.

> "My only experience on TV came as a contestant on The Price is Right."

When we finally entered the studio people started pushing to find a seat. A few were running up and down the aisles as if the show would start without them. I overheard a couple

Diner Lingo Quiz

Which of these is "not" a way to order water in diner lingo?
a. Mississippi mud
b. Adam's ale
c. City juice
d. Dog soup

Answer Chap 11

14

of the girls from the airline say they thought someone in our group might be picked. Wow, that would be wonderful—as long as it wasn't me. Not me. Nope. Please, not me.

Everyone was finally seated and the theme song played. Applause signs began flashing and Bob Barker himself stepped out onto the stage. Okay, maybe this would be fun. Folks were laughing and yelling and acting pretty silly. Names were called, one after another, and audience members ran down to the stage.

Then it happened. My name! Bob Barker was calling my name. "Arlene Johnson, come on down." What? Arlene Johnson? I go by my middle name, Renae! Nonetheless, he meant me.

My friends jumped up and down, but I couldn't move my feet. Again, my name was called. Bob Barker was calling my name. So, finally, like all the other contestants, I ran down the aisle waving my arms.

I was mortified. I didn't know how to play the games, but I smiled and tried to stop the voices in my head that were urging me to run. The first game was with contestants who hadn't made it on stage yet. Win there, and you get to go up on stage.

So the guessing began. How much does this or that cost? You can't go over. All I wanted to do was to go back to my seat, but Bob Barker kept bringing more stuff out. Finally, there was a beautiful brass telescope on an oak stand. Bob Barker looked straight at me and I heard his words echo: "How much do you think it retails for without going over? Arlene?" I felt panicked so I looked out over the sea of crazy folks behind me yelling out prices, and all I could hear was one man shouting, "$1400." Okay, fine. "$1400," I said, and the next thing I knew – I was on stage. Yep! Cameras, lights, and Bob Barker. But the worst part was: There were more games! During commercial breaks, Mr. Barker would have his face powdered and speak to me, but all I could think about were the games.

> "My friends jumped up and down, but I couldn't move my feet."

I didn't understand them, so I just smiled and smiled and smiled. Somehow, I made it through even more games and reached the big wheel, the final showcase. One big spin of the wheel and it was over. I was back in my seat and able to breathe again. Soon I was on the flight home. The $1450 telescope would arrive in a few weeks.

You are probably wondering what I did with that telescope. I took it to a camera shop in Scottsdale, Arizona. They wanted it to display in the front window and said that they would let me know if they got an offer. A few months later, a check arrived for $1255.

So that was my big television experience, and not one I had dreams of repeating.

It wasn't too many months before I was called back to my work as a flight attendant for America West. Even though flight attendants are there for emergencies, most folks think that they are there to serve food and drinks. I served coffee, cold drinks, snacks, sandwiches—with a smile.

In 1996, my husband, Phil, got a call from a dear friend, Bill Gaither. He wanted us to move back to Nashville and Phil take the position of A & R Director for his record company "Springhill Music Group". The move to Nashville made commuting to Phoenix and America West very difficult. So, when Larry Black in 1998 called looking for a receptionist, I decided to retire my wings. I went to work for Larry at Gabriel Communications. He had just produced his first Country's Family Reunion, and it was a huge success. Thanks to my cross-training with the airlines, especially in customer service, reservations and my ability and willingness to serve him coffee ... pretty much got me the job. Over the years my receptionist job came to include the roles of office manager, personal assistant, assistant bookkeeper, warehouse and shipping clerk, customer service supervisor, and marketing all roll up into VP of Operations. I could say the rest is history but I am sure you are wondering how I got this wonderful TV waitress gig. It's very simple.

One morning Larry walked in my office, sat down and said he had an idea for a new show. A talk show but not the conventional behind the desk ... interview type show. He then shared his DINER show idea and the cast of characters which included me.

And now I can say that the rest is history. By day I work in his office and by TV I work in his Diner. But whether it is at the office or on TV it's pretty much the same ... A WHOLE LOT OF FUN.

3

Sassy Diner Attire

My only experience wearing a uniform was when I was a flight attendant. I wore the required airline-issue basic navy skirt, pin-striped shirt, matching tailored jacket and tie. On my left shoulder, I wore my wings and nametag. Panty hose and navy pumps completed the outfit. What I disliked most about my professional attire is it meant I had to check in every month to be weighed. Not one pound could be hidden in this form-fitting polyester uniform.

All the flight attendants agreed that the most glamorous part of the job was the stroll through the airport dressed in our sharp outfits and dragging our matching luggage. Once on the aircraft, I looked forward to shedding the navy tailored jacket for my service apron. I wore a very special bib apron with my name embroidered on it. It was official: I looked like a waitress.

When I went to work for Larry Black, there was no required uniform. In fact, jeans and tennis shoes were standard. Serving coffee in the office certainly didn't require a special apron.

In 2009, when Larry announced we were creating a new television show for RFD-TV and that it would be set in a diner, and that I would be the waitress, I had flashbacks of my airline bib apron. After further brainstorming, he decided it would be a country diner. And he wanted it to feel like a country diner in Middle America, where country folks could enjoy good home-style cooking with live entertainment, and be served by a smart-mouth waitress. Okay, so that meant special sassy attire. I could do that! I began to do some research on diners and the history of diner waitress fashions.

There have been many styles over the years. The diner waitress uniform became popular in the 1950s and 1960s and could be found all across the nation. The vintage waitress uniforms typically consisted of a dress with collar and pockets. They came in a simple style that was comfortable enough to stand a long workday.

Here are some of the basic styles:

The Basic Diner Dress was made of cotton/polyester, often in a solid color (such as pink or blue) with a contrasting white trim on the sleeves and collar. It usually buttoned up the front and had plenty of pockets for an order pad, pen and other stuff. This look has been worn since the 50s, in coffee and ice cream shops also.

The Diner Uniform was double-breasted with short sleeves, cuffs and side pockets. Most had an elastic waist for better fit and comfort. The apron included scallops and a tie in the back.

Diner Lingo Quiz

What would a cook do if you told him to "make it cry?"
a. Cook it rare
b. Cook it well-done
c. Add onions
d. Add water

Answer: Chap 11

26

The Soda Uniform was a bright color, such as red accented with white or a checkered pattern. It was a more youthful look.

No vintage waitress uniform was complete without the proper accessories: an order pad, pencil, nametag and serving tray. Many waitresses wore hairnets to keep hair out of their faces as well as the customer's food.

Over the next few years, more fast-food chain eateries appeared, and the mom and pop diners disappeared. In today's restaurants we have "servers." I was recently in Las Vegas and met a server who actually had a handheld computer into which she entered our order, which was then sent directly to the kitchen without her moving from our table. Wow! "No order pad, pencil, nametag or serving tray. Who was that girl and what did she do with our waitress?"

The interesting (or perhaps not so interesting) decision as to what the waitress on Larry's Country Diner, being me, should wear was never made. Larry ordered a few shirts for himself and a tan butcher apron. He ordered me a few matching shirts to consider. I thought they looked pretty nice. One was navy, one green and one black; they were V-neck shirts with our logo. I knew I didn't want to wear a bib-style butcher apron to match Larry's, so I searched for a white diner waitress- style apron. I found what I wanted and added some lace. I sewed on our logo and had my apron.

By the time Larry started scheduling our first week of tapings, I was pretty sure we were going to have long days. The "country" aspect had to be represented in my uniform, but my research kept bringing me back to those skimpy Vegas–style outfits. And that sure wasn't gonna happen. (In fact, there should be an age restriction on those types of outfits. You know the ones I am talking about.) So I took a look at some wholesome cowgirl outfits and there I found my long skirt and boots. Voila! My Larry's Country Diner Waitress one-of-a-kind waiting on tables outfit. And it works for me!

Now, I am not saying I haven't tried different combinations, but I pretty much stuck with the same comfortable flowing skirt, cloth boots and diner logo shirt. I did trade my long skirt for a pair of jeans on a couple of shows, but I received letters asking me what had happened to my flowing skirt! I was so happy anyone noticed that I stuck to my skirt ever after.

To complete my attire, I made some Larry's Country Diner logo earrings with a matching necklace. In addition to my bottle cap earrings, I have made Jimmy Capp's guitar pick and diner fork earrings. All just fun stuff from the diner.

After several seasons, we were very fortunate to include Boot Daddy (PFI Western Wear) to our sponsorship lineup. And with that came some very nice perks. On one of our shows, Paul from Boot Daddy presented me with a pair of brown boots with a cool cross on them. On another show, Nadine and I received cowboy hats!

It's fun being a Country Diner TV waitress!!!

That's No Waitress

Several artists on our television show have come through my swinging door and asked to help serve the Diner patrons. And a few actually surprised (even) Larry!

On season one, country legend Jan Howard was the first to help me wait on tables. She was by far the most experienced waitress on our show and actually had me worried she might take over my job. She was a natural, a classy-looking waitress you would hope to see in any diner across America. Jan not only served our customers lunch like a pro, she actually sang to them. When she sat down at a table next to a couple of the guys, their faces turned beet red. One guy got his bald head rubbed. It's funny how guys talk big until they are confronted by a good lookin' female. Of course, the whole Diner was laughing. Jan felt so comfortable in her apron, she wore it for the whole show with Bill Anderson. I told her that I might be calling when I need help on the show.

The most unexpected help I had following me through the kitchen door was William Lee Golden of the Oak Ridge Boys.

He not only surprised Larry and the Diner guests, the "press" on hand went into shock. The gray-haired, tall, good-looking baritone who doesn't mince words was carrying a tray and serving food. As I tied an apron around his waist, mouths in the Diner dropped open and flash bulbs went off. It really was a sight to behold. I think he had as much fun as we did, and actually made a repeat visit.

What can I say about Larry Gatlin! He doesn't even need an apron. He will grab my tray of food and bust through the kitchen door on a whim, invited or not. And he brings new meaning to "Where the cameras are always rollin', and we don't care." We have had folks send us letters asking why Larry Gatlin gets to come on the show and try and take over. He doesn't! He just LOVES country music and the folks that make it. He really cannot help himself. He is a natural performer and so quick.

> *"It's funny how guys talk big until they are confronted by a good lookin' female."*

A lot of the time he leaves even Larry Black speechless. I am a huge fan of the Gatlin Brothers and will share my kitchen with Larry G. any time. So look out if you are in the Diner and Larry Gatlin is there. He may grab you up for a dance or share your cup of coffee.

Another Larry that felt right at home coming through the kitchen door was Larry Mahan. What a gentleman, which surprised me for such a macho, bull-riding, all-American

31

cowboy! He actually went looking for an apron before it was even time for the show and asked where the kitchen door was. I wish we had served steak sandwiches in the Diner that day, just in his honor. I did remember to wear my cowboy hat and boots. By the end of the day, my feet were killing me! So much for cowgirl waitressing.

Buddy Greene was another acquaintance that wore a Diner apron. Buddy is known in the Christian music field and has performed a lot on the Gaither Homecoming series. He is an amazing musician and songwriter. And, of course, the song he co-wrote with Mark Lowry called "Mary Did You Know?" is a Christmas favorite. He is always fun to have on the Diner, and we all know Bill Gaither doesn't let him wear an apron on his show! He was a member of Jerry Reed's band, and I feel sure Jerry would have let him wear one just for the fun of it. After all, "When you're hot, you're hot."

I have to admit that I did make my daughter, Chi, dress up in an apron and go through the kitchen door unexpected. Well, not exactly unexpected: She was expecting. 8½ months to be exact. And through the door I sent her, balancing a tray on her stomach. Larry started laughing and the guys from Exile all gasped. But in her defense, it was for me! As you may or may not know, she is a professional dancer and choreographer living in Nashville now . Most folks have no idea of the work that entails. She could be working on a TV show, commercial, stage show, industrial, movie, convention or tour. And working is what she was doing all 8½ months, and it made me a little nervous. When you have to take a doctor's note to board a plane, that is a little too much work.

Southern Style
FRIED CHICKEN
French Fries and Salad
"You'll Really Enjoy this treat!"

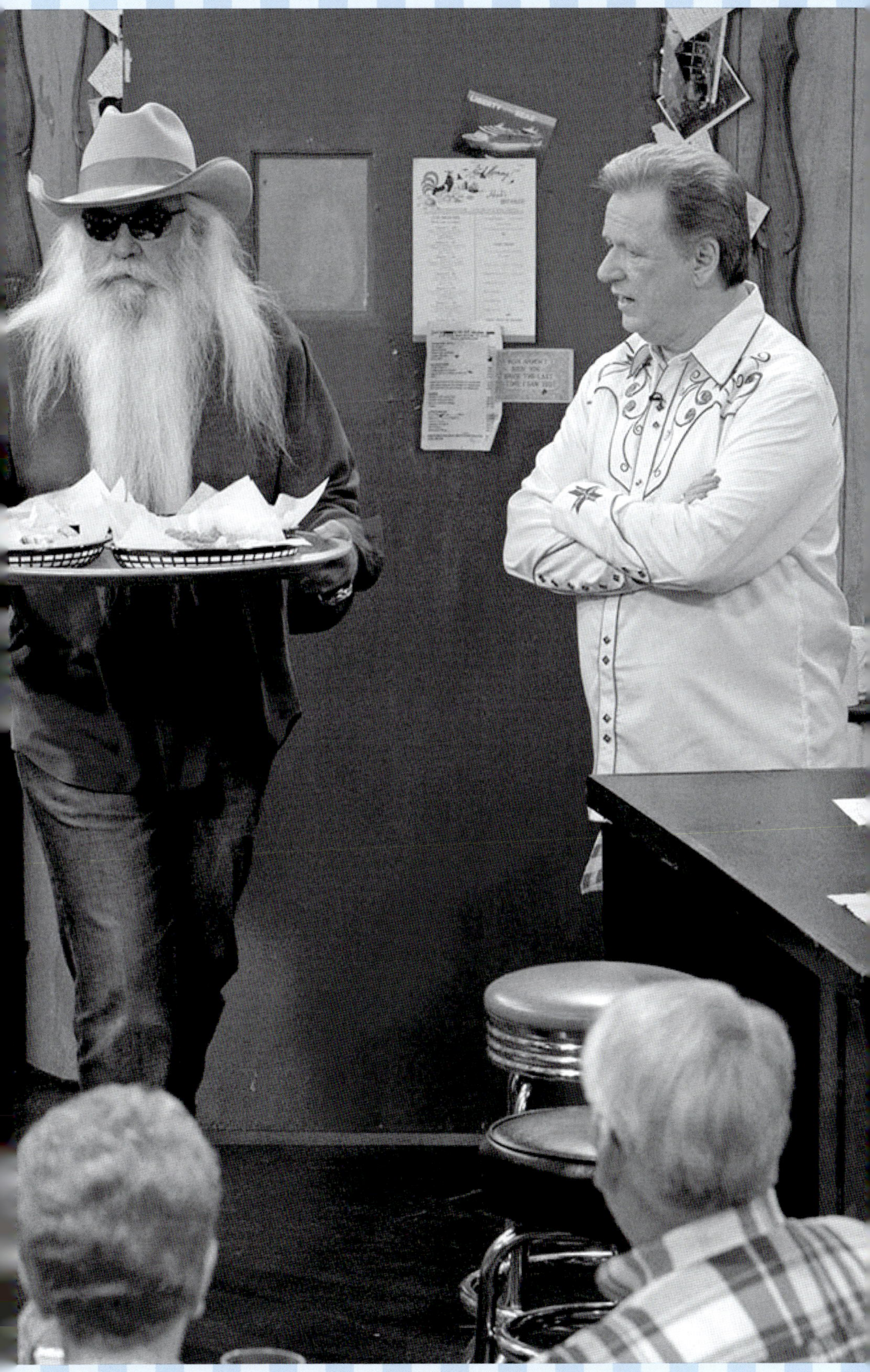

The weekend before our Diner taping, her husband, being the good husband he is, drove her five hours to St Louis where she had choreographed a show for Dollar General with William Shatner. Star Trek or not, that was it! No more. She could actually have had our granddaughter on the road. So I asked her to come to our Diner tapings just to keep an eye on her! I was getting tired checking my phone on the counter. And being the fun-loving waitress I am, who loves to surprise Larry, I couldn't resist tying an apron over her huge belly and sending her through the door.

Diner Lingo Quiz

What is a "Joe O'Malley?"
A. Eggs and toast
B. Corned beef
C. Irish coffee
D. Grilled cheese with ham

Answer Chap 11

5

Squeaky Door

When the Diner set was created, it was given two doors. One, of course, was the side door with the bell hanging above it that rings when Nadine enters. The second was the swinging kitchen door I use.

Of course, when we first saw our Diner set, we thought that Nadine's door with the bell would be the most fun. You know, the bell ringing when folks go in and out. In reality, that door is the actual entrance to the diner, with an open and closed sign on it. Folks coming to eat at Larry's Country Diner would come in and out. As it turned out, during our tapings, folks would get seated and never leave. And once Nadine walked through the door no one could hear the bell. To our surprise my swinging door took on a squeaky charm and character of its own and received the most attention.

During our first season, the door was the subject of tons of mail. And not all positive. The door had this LOUD squeak. As I would go in and out, in and out, bringing in food from the kitchen, the door's squeak would get louder and louder.

Diner Lingo Quiz

What is "butcher's revenge?"
A. Steak
B. Undercooked hamburger
C. Buffalo chicken
D. Meat loaf

Answer: Chap 11

38

By the end of the day and our last taping of the day, it was so loud that the cameras' audio was picking up the sound. No matter how many times I tried to enter S L O W L Y, it squeaked. I even tried to time my entrance while the artist were performing, hoping the music would drown out the noise.

The guys in the sound booth finally had enough. They found the maintenance crew and had them grease the hinges. But Larry was not happy. He loved that squeak. He contends, "It's those quirky real life things on the set that make it feel like a real diner. If you walk into a real mom and pop diner in Middle America, they would probably have a squeaky kitchen door." So, with some compromise arrangements, it now squeaks a little.

If you have never been behind the scenes of a "set" design, it's pretty amazing. I'll give you my version of it. Movies, stage shows, commercials–almost anything you see on television—are on sets. There is usually one huge room with a room created inside that room, and it looks like you are framing a house. Outside the set room are cameras, lighting, electrical equipment and so on. I call them booby traps. You have to watch where you step and stand.

> *"If you have never been behind the scenes of a "set" design, it's pretty amazing."*

And there are usually guys running around checking stuff all the time, making sure everything is working properly. A couple of shows, my big coffee maker was not plugged in. To plug it in there has to be an electrical cord through the set wall that connects to another large electrical cord that connects to a live electric outlet somewhere in the actual building. I have learned to always check it before the show.

Phil Johnson, my husband, is our photographer. You have heard Larry refer to him as being on a ladder somewhere. That is exactly true. He spends most of the day on top of an 8-foot ladder, either behind the cameras or on the side of the set, looking over the set walls through a camera lens. He has gotten some priceless shots of the artists, but he has also captured the heart of the Diner through his photography. We have been able to use his pictures in magazines, press releases, packaging, newspapers and commercials for both Country's Family Reunion and Larry's Country Diner.

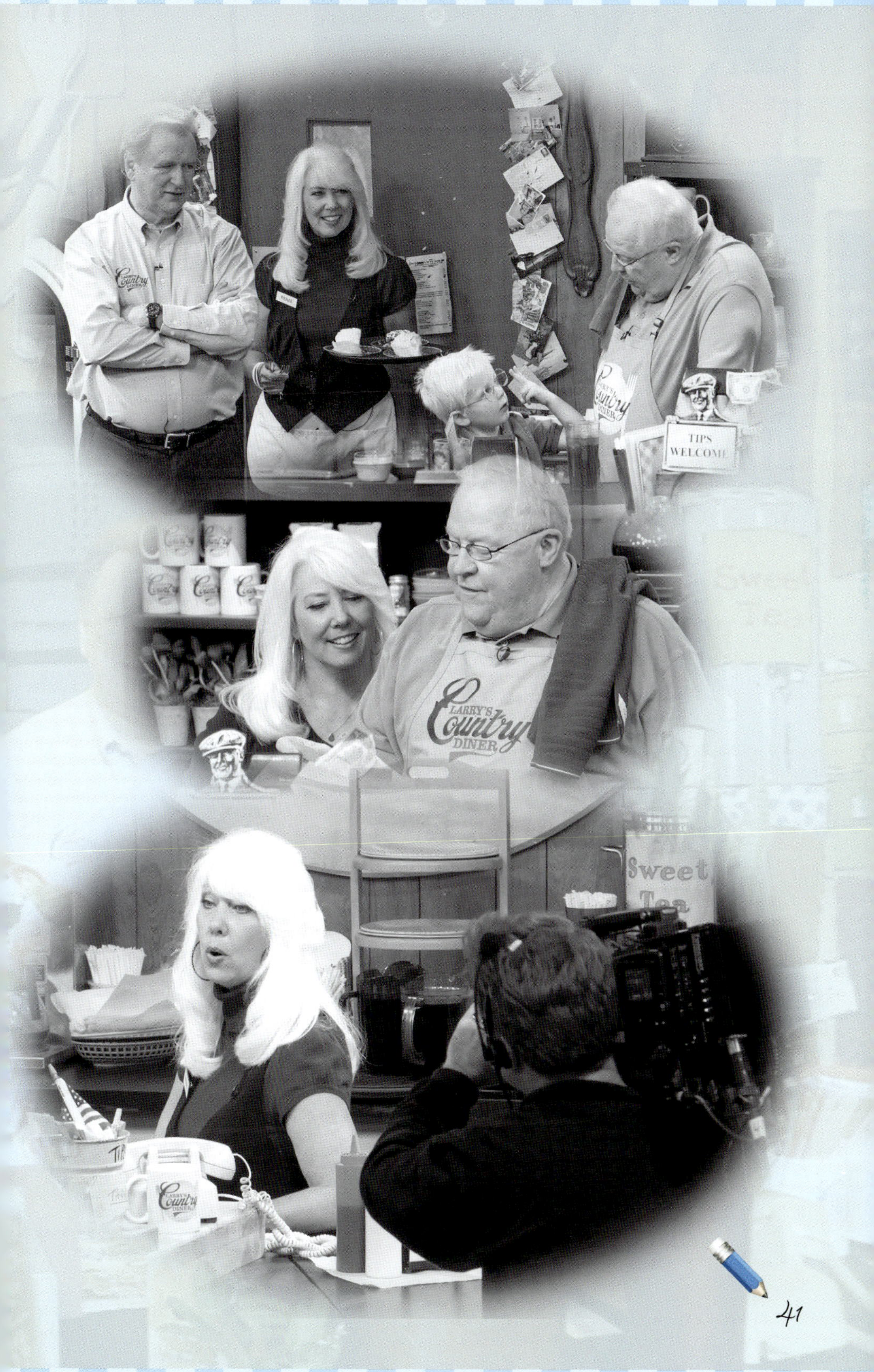
TIPS
WELCOME
LARRY'S
Country
DINER
Sweet
Tea

TV Diner Jokes

Q: Where do burgers like to dance?
A: At a meat ball!

Q: Why did the man climb to the roof of the fast food restaurant?
A: They told him the meal was on the house!

Q: When can a hamburger marry a hot dog?
A: After they have a very frank relationship!

"This isn't Burger King"

Diners usually have *Daily Specials* on their menus. But what I serve at the Diner rarely changes. In fact, we tell our guests, "This isn't Burger King. You can't have it your way." Our menu consists of a club sandwich with chips, chicken fingers with cold slaw, and a hamburger with fries. And the folks in the Diner have no say as to what I am serving them. We call it TV food and no one seems to mind. In fact, hot food, a good piece of pie, a glass of sweet tea and great entertainment is about as good as it gets.

A lot of folks have asked if our food is real. Yep! It is cooked fresh during the show, around the corner from my swinging door in a makeshift kitchen. It's usually hot and very tasty. The trick is to get the food served to everyone in the Diner (plus tea, coffee and our famous desserts) before the show has finished taping or the food gets cold. I have learned to carry a tray with several plates of food and maneuver around the counter, camera cords and crowded tables pretty well. But I do have the occasional fork dropping or knife sliding off the tray. And Larry loves to stop the show and point that out, of course. I've always known he has a sick sense of humor!

Keith has this ever-tempting urge to interrupt my service. He has been known to hold the swinging door, not allowing me to come through. This can cause quite a tug of war, which usually gets Larry's attention and cues him to have some fun. During one show, Keith literally dumped a tray of silverware and blamed me, just to cause a ruckus! Once he took a French fry off a plate while I was serving and ate it! Yuck! THAT did cause me concern! Who wants to be served a plate of food Keith has eaten from? Yeah, yeah. I know he is a famous announcer from the Grand Ole Opry and knows every famous country music legend, but do you want him eating off your plate?

> *"... he has been known to take a bite of a customer's hamburger."*

When Larry Gatlin is on the show, it seems like a free-for-all. He once grabbed Larry's Redneck Sweet Tea Glass and started adding packages of sugar to it. This was funny but the tea was unfit to drink! And he has been known to take a bite of a customer's hamburger.

But the two who fight the most over food are Larry and Nadine. It doesn't matter how many times I serve Nadine chocolate pudding with a red cherry on the top. Larry grabs the cherry and pops it into his mouth. It's like waving a red towel in front of a bull. I don't know if Larry really likes cherries that much, but he does like getting on Nadine's bad side.

DINER QUIZ

What would you get if your waitress said to "Twist it, choke it, and make it cackle?"

a. Sausage, hash, and eggs
b. A chocolate malt with egg
c. Twist ice cream with sprinkles
d. Add lettuce and tomatoes

Answer: Chap 11

45

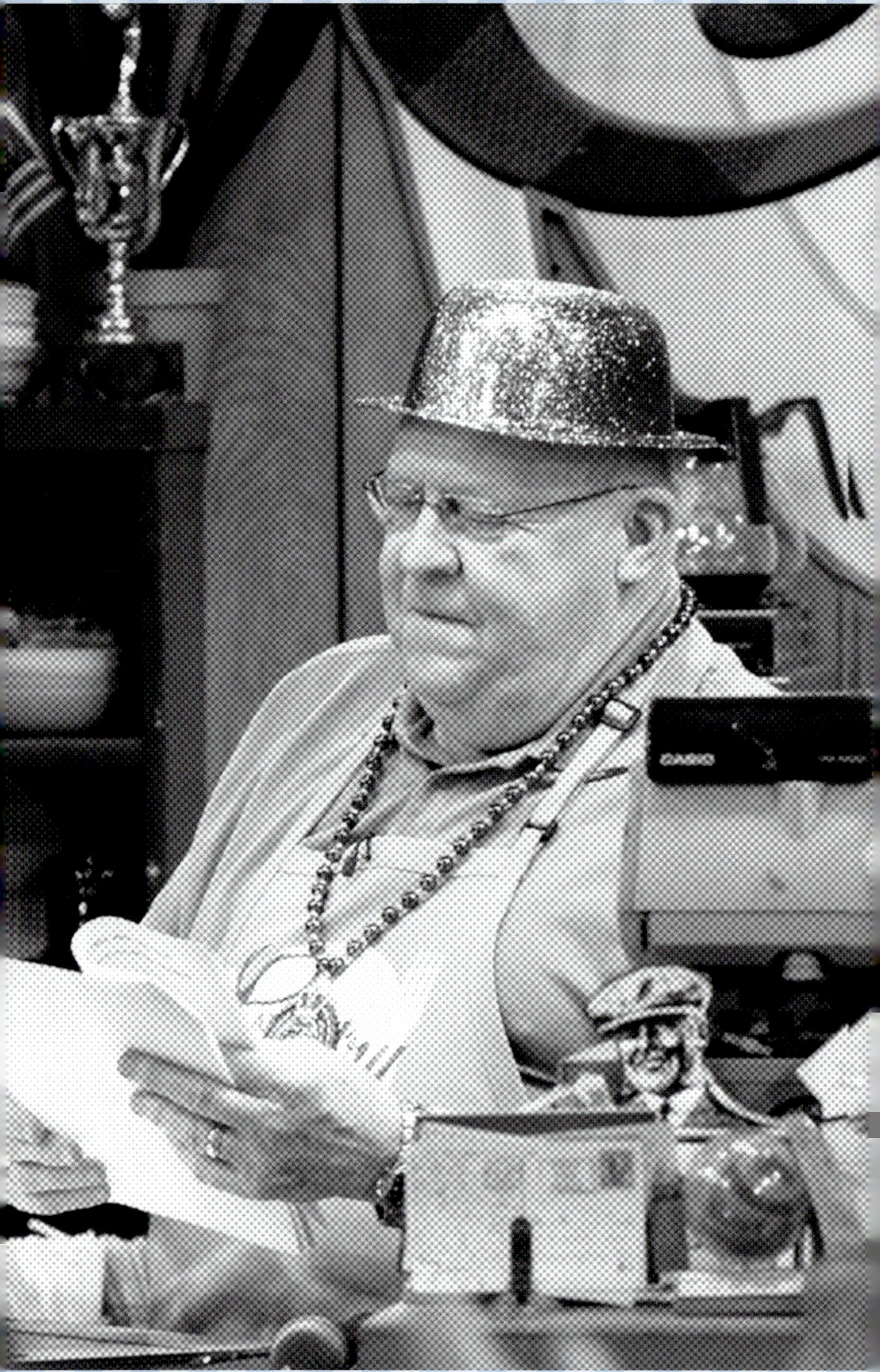

DINER

DINER QUIZ

What would you get if you ordered a "family reunion?"
a. Hot dog and fries
b. Chocolate & vanilla ice cream
c. Orange juice and toast
d. Chicken and egg sandwich

Answer: Chap 11

The most *famous* mishap and the one we received the most mail about, Larry initiated. I was walking from the back of the Diner carrying several baskets I had cleared off the tables. My tray was full of leftover French fries with ketchup, chicken fingers and even a pie someone hadn't finished eating. (I know, who wouldn't eat all of their pie?) As I rounded the counter and headed for the kitchen door, I happened to look up at Larry. And there it was--that mischievous look out of the corner of his eye, that smile that says, "*This is going to be good.*" Then it happened, so fast I barely had time to react. Just as I got within reach, Larry leaned back and with a quick hand flipped my tray. Food started flying! I tried to steady the tray, holding it close to my chest so the food would fall against me. But it was too late. Keith saw his chance and, like lightening, he was there putting in the additional shove that allowed everything on the tray to land on the floor behind the counter. Immediately Scotty, being the great cameraman he is, was right there filming my reaction. Sooooooo, I did what any seasoned TV waitresses would do: I picked up a few of the French fries off the floor and began throwing them at Larry and Keith. A real Diner food fight! Larry was laughing, while our special guests, Exile, were ducking. And it was all caught on camera and broadcast on TV. Like we say at the Diner, "Where the cameras are always rollin', and we don't care." But I did get a letter from a customer who said that we had set a poor example for kids taught not to throw their food. I did apologize, but Larry just laughed.

On a few occasions, food has been served late. I try and gage when the show will start or, as we say in the business,

"Roll tape." But there can be all kinds of delays. The audio may need adjusting, which happens frequently due to the fact we have so many microphones and headsets. The camera guys may need to get different angle instructions, and sometimes the lighting overhead may need tweaking. Other delays could be caused by the control booth and tape machines, or the makeup artists who find we need extra powder on our shiny noses or bald spots.

On one show, Guy Gilchrist was sitting in the Diner. He is the famous cartoonist who created the "Nancy" comic strip and worked with Jim Henson and the Muppets. A friend of Keith, he just stopped by. The show started and things had been going pretty smoothly in the Diner. Or so I thought. That is, until Larry decided to take a stroll to Guy's table. I was busy filling coffee cups, not paying too much attention, until I heard those dreaded words, "Yeah, but the food is cold and it takes forever to get served." I stopped in my tracks. Larry knew something was going to happen. It didn't take me two seconds before I was back through those swinging doors with plates and plates of HOT food and pie, more than he could possibly eat. Guy just smiled and Larry of course was laughing. You don't mess with the waitress!

Of course, most waitresses don't have the luxury of having so much fun with so- called complaints. For them it becomes a nightmare, a real liability. So what do I advise other waitress to do? Nothing. Just laugh and go with it.

The Counter

Behind the Counter is an interesting place. The actual counter has no drawers or shelves. It's a hollow opening held in place with sandbags. Otherwise, it would surely slide with Larry pulling on it. The space under the counter is very convenient. We store props and signs that may be needed during the show there. The collection of "not our sponsor" signs found a good home there, along with our CRUISE signs. We usually gather a collection of CD's, DVD's, books or anything else the guest artists may bring to promote.

We have actually hidden people behind our counter. Scotty, our camera guy, spends a lot of time behind the counter. You will rarely see him, but he gets those close camera shots of Nadine that are priceless. He is our "up close and personal" cameraman. Sometimes, you don't even know he is there until you feel a big cold camera lens by your nose or you trip over his camera cord.

For one show, Darrin Vincent had dropped by to visit the Diner. So Keith came up with the idea to hide him behind the counter. The plan was to have him laugh on cue, once we came back from commercial break. The scheduled artist was told to open his mouth as if he were laughing, but it would be Darrin laughing. Darrin's laugh is so recognizable and funny that we were certain the TV audience would figure it out! However, when it came time for Darrin to laugh on "cue," he couldn't—or, at least, what came out of his mouth didn't sound like laughter. Larry and I looked at Darrin as if to say, "What was that?" And you know the rest of the story. We died laughing, belly laughing. And that was all it took for Darrin. Darrin's infectious laugh kicked in and we were all laughing our heads off. I am still not sure our TV audience thought it was that hysterical, but for us it was just another day at the Diner having fun.

I am always having to pull stuff from underneath the counter while we are on the air, Larry's red towel (when he forgets to wear it) or fan gifts that we want to show to our TV audience. It's a safe place for large breakable items or collectables, like the Chuck Connors rifle presented to us and the signed sketch of George Jones we plan to hang in our REAL Diner. But, Lord, don't put anything down there that Larry hasn't seen. He is so nosey! If he sees anything under there he doesn't recognize, he might just pull it out during the show and ask me what it is. And not everything needs to be seen. He's always screwing up my mail segment!

The counter itself holds a lot of "stuff." There is the tip jar (that rarely receives a tip), our *menu* (with clever food titles like *Jim Ed's Brown Gravy)*, our *phone* (that never rings), our *cash register* (that never opens) and our *mail holder*. Our mail includes not only entertaining emails and letters, which I

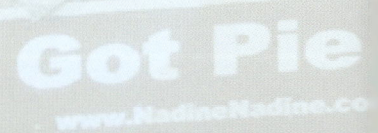

Behind the Counter

Front of Counter

On top of counter

occasionally read, but also postcards. On my kitchen door, there are postcards attached to the doorframe, props actually. However, the postcards I receive from our fans are saved. Those postcards are to be attached to the doorframes at our real Larry's Country Diner in Nashville, Tennessee. We hope some day folks will come to visit the Diner and look for their postcards.

Larry's Redneck Sweet Tea Glass is a **must** on the counter. Usually, when Larry starts the *Day in History* or the *Year in History* segment, he wants a sip of sweet tea. I don't know if he thinks his mouth will get dry from reading or if it's just a habit, but he has to have his tea. And Larry can't have a regular glass! So being the super duper TV waitress I am, I started my own line of "redneck glasses" for our show. They are called "Redneck Classy Glasses." Larry's tea glass is a 32 oz (quart size) mason jar on a glass stem. It's big enough to hold all the sweet tea he can drink during the show. And it's a very special glass. It not only comes with a lid that keeps your drink from spillin'. It has an autographed photo of Larry on the lid, our signature bottle cap logo hanging from the glass stem, and THE PROMISE on the tag.

Now, speaking of *The Promise*, that is another special item that sits on the counter. *The Promise* cards are in a box from which Larry pulls each show's promise in order. But he rarely puts them back like he should. That results in him grabbing the same promise and reading it again. He, of course, looks at me like I have sabotaged him. So I try and shuffle them every so often.

Diner Lingo Quiz

What do you think "belly chokers" refer to?
a. Doughnuts
b. Sausage
c. Liver
d. Alka seltzer

Answer Chap 11

55

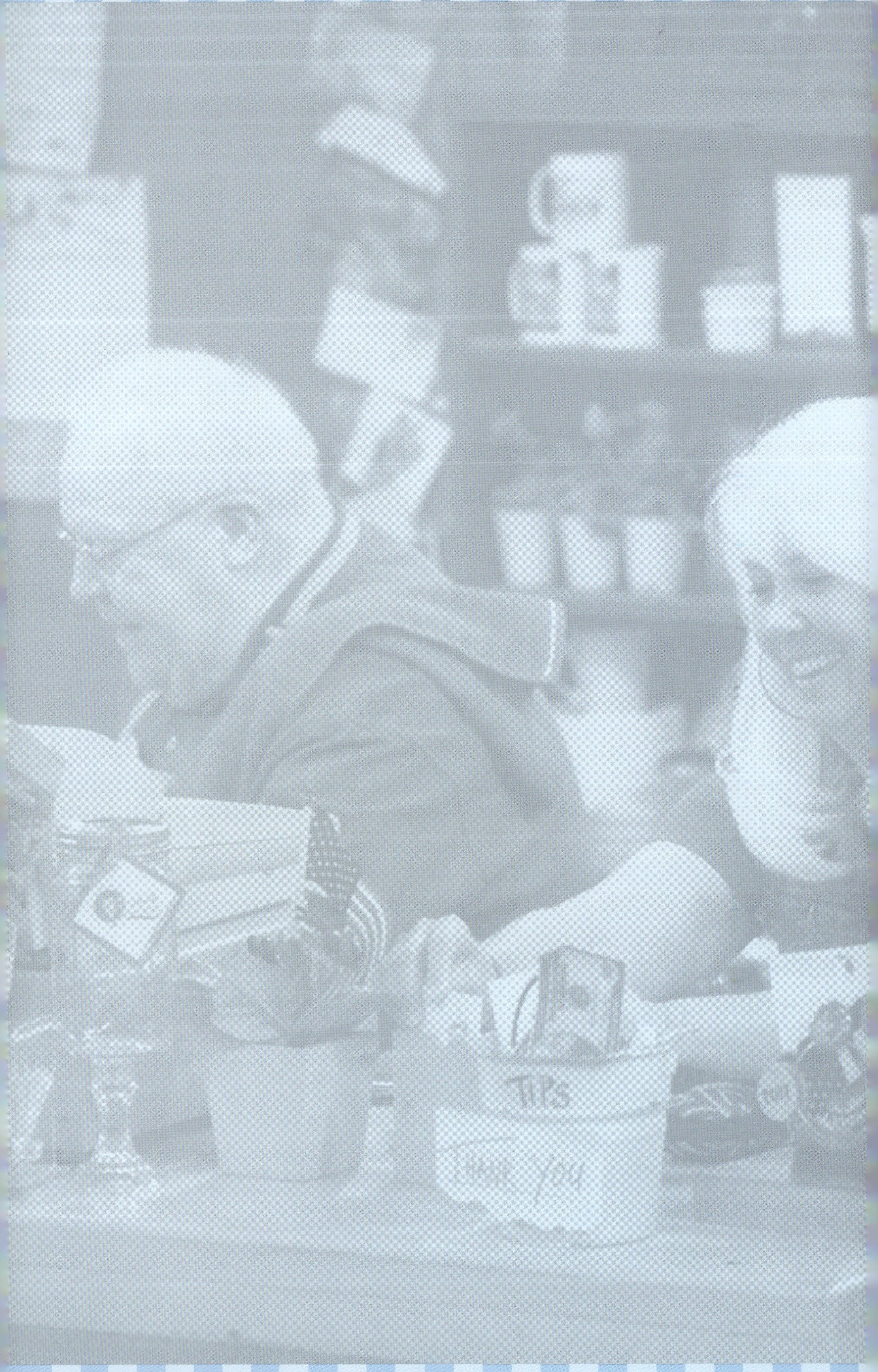
TIPS
Thank You

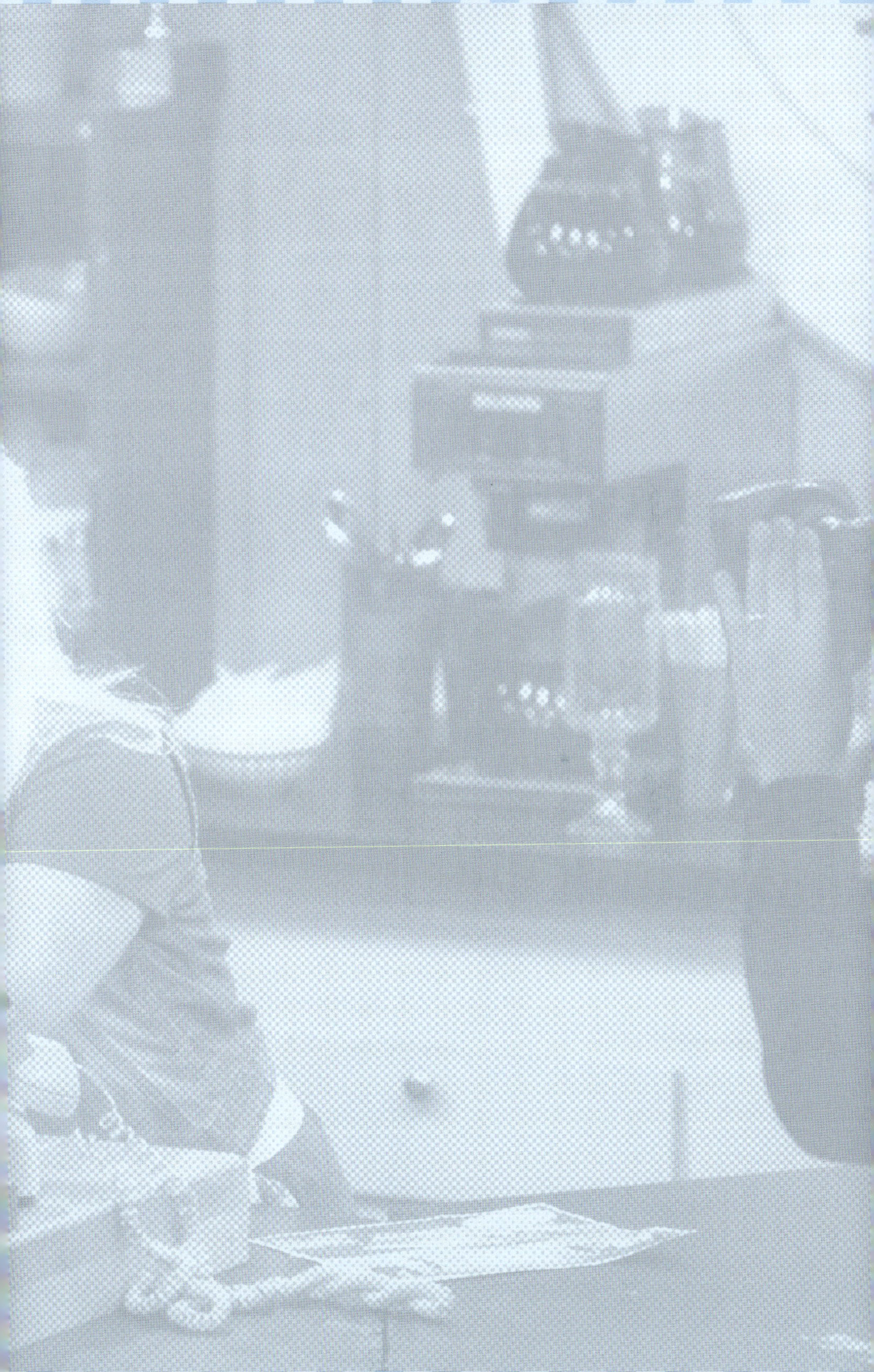

HOT FUDGE SUNDAE
PIE a la MODE
PECAN
APPLE
STRAWBERRY
ICE CREAM SODAS
Southern Style
FRIED CHICKEN
French Fries and Salad
LARRY'S Country DINER

A little history about our counter. When the show started, we had a larger counter. It was longer and curved out more. On some of our early shows, the artists would just sit down at it. They could talk to Larry and occasionally sneak a few bites of pie. Several of them sang from the counter. For me it was great. I actually had room to walk around them. I rarely got between them and the camera, and I was able to served that side of the diner very easily. THEN Larry decided we were going to try and do a Larry's Country Diner stage show in Branson at the RFD Theater.

That trip proved to be a problem for the counter. So we ended up creating a smaller one. The new counter was the perfect size for stage shows at the Starlite Theater as well as our cruise ship performances. The counter could be assembled and disassembled and transported easily. NICE. However, all of a sudden I didn't have the same space around the end of the counter for serving. I was bumping into Keith at the end of the counter and suddenly I was invading the performance space. Who would think a few inches of counter space would make such a difference? But it does. I find myself moving Keith out of the way and going around the other side of the counter. It also takes a few more steps but, hey, I am a TV waitress!

There is a very special spot at our counter. It is saved for our very special church lady, NADINE. She has her own padded stool, which she climbs up on. And once she gets adjusted, she plops her purse and oversized Bible on the counter. It's convenient for Larry to talk with her there and easy for me to serve her dessert. She also has a perfect view of the artists. The counter feels a little empty until she arrives, but once she is there the Diner counter is complete.

TV Diner Jokes

Q: How do you make a hamburger smile?

A: Pickle it gently!

Q: Did you hear about the hamburger who couldn't stop making jokes?

A: He was on a roll!

Q: What are the best days of the week in FastFoodland?

A: Fry-day and Sundae!

Got Pie?

Who doesn't love pie?? Pie makes you think of family gatherings, church socials and home. On our TV show, you will see me actually serving some of our delicious pie to our guests in the Diner. I've had folks say, "Just skip the meal and bring me some of that pie!!"

If there ever was a person who loved sweets more than NADINE then I haven't met them. Every show she is ready for some pie as soon as she sits down. And if I don't serve it to her fast enough, you will hear her say, "Renae, you got any pie left?"

The funny thing about Nadine is that she literally eats a piece of pie every show. By the end of the day she has consumed 4 pieces, not to mention the dessert she eats during our lunch break with the cast and crew. I do give her some variety by serving, lemon, chocolate, coconut cream, pecan, and an occasional pudding sundae. When Nadine decided to write a cookbook, it only made sense that it be a Dessert Cookbook.

And the title fit perfectly, Dessert Is Like Heaven, You Don't Want To Miss It.

When we are on the road with our shows at the Starlite Theater and on our Larry's Country Diner and Country's Family Reunion Cruises, I still serve folks on stage. We usually have six tables that seat 21 folks from our audience. Since we don't have a kitchen to cook in, we opted for pie only. Pie and a good cup of coffee and great entertainment!

My mom was known for her fabulous pies. She knew just how to roll out a crust and fill it with the perfect mixture before adding a golden Meringue. My mom was one of those cooks that never measure ingredients. She just knew by looking. She made coconut crème for my dad, lime meringue for my husband, chocolate for me, and pineapple for my brother. There were many times we asked for a pie instead of a birthday cake. And if you were ever sick, I swear, one of her pies would heal you. In April of 2013, my mom passed away and in her honor we served pies.

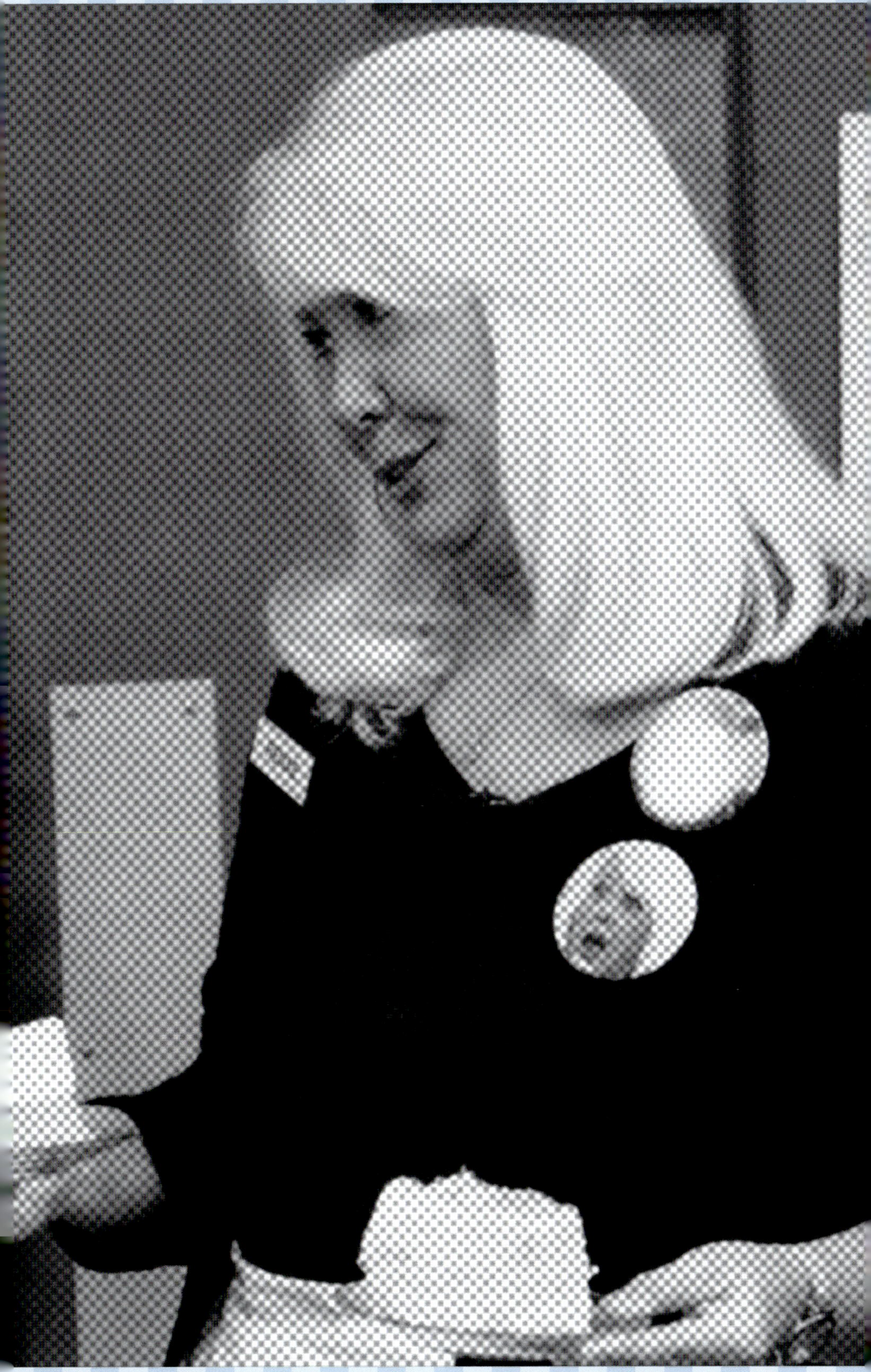

Diner Lingo Quiz

Which of these is "not" a way to order milk in diner lingo?
a. Cow juice
b. Balloon juice
c. Baby juice
d. Moo juice

Answer: Chap 11

64

65

Guest Check

Mom's Lemon Meringue Pie

Lemon Filling:
¾ cup Cornstarch, ½ cup lemon juice, 3 tablespoons flour
1 tablespoon lemon peel, grated, 1-¾ cups sugar
1-tablespoon butter, 1/3 teaspoon salt, 2 cups water
4 egg yolks, slightly beaten, *Baked pie shell

Combine cornstarch, flour, sugar and salt mixing well. Gradually add water, stirring until smooth over a medium heat. Bring to a boil and quickly stir some of the hot mixture into yolks then pour back into hot mixture: stir to blend. Return to heat and cook on low for 5 minutes. Remove from heat: stir in lemon juice, lemon peel, and butter. Pour into pie shell. Preheat oven to 400 degrees

Meringue:
4 egg whites, ½ cup of sugar, ½ tsp cream of tarter

With mixture on medium speed beat whites and cream of tarter until frothy. Gradually add sugar 2 tablespoons at a time. Beat a high speed until stiff peaks. Spread meringue over lemon filling. Bake 7-9 minutes or until the meringue is golden brown.
Let cool ... serves 8.

Mom

Aaron Tippin

Bill Anderson

Baillie & The Boys

Bobby Bare

The Bellamy Bros

Bill Medley

Billy Dean

Billy Grammer

BJ Thomas

LaDonna Gatlin

Buddy Greene & Ben Isaac

Con Hunley

Cleverlys

Collin Raye

The Church Sisters

Johnny Counterfit

Dailey & Vincent

Doyle Lawson

Dan & Hannah Miller

Exile

Ed Bruce

Eddy Raven

Barbara Fairchild

Gary Chapman

Gary Morris

Gene Watson

Georgette Jones

Gordon Mote

Guy Penrod

William Lee Golden

Helen Cornelius

Hot Club of Cowtown

James Gregory

Jamie O'Neal

Jan Howard

Jarrett Garrett

Jean Shepard

Jim Menzies

Jim Glaser

Jim Lauderdale

Jimmy C Newman

Jimmy Fortune

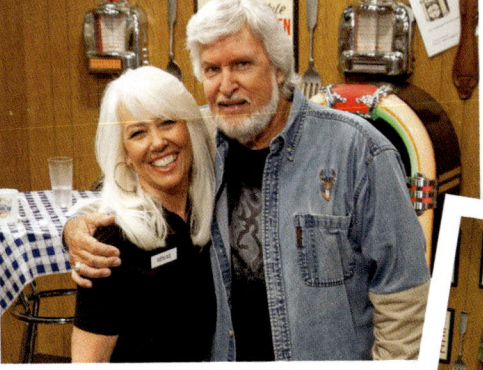

Joe Stamply

Joey, Rory & Heidi

John Anderson

John Conlee

Johnny Rodriguez

Larry Gatlin

Hoot Hester & Larry Mahan

Larry & Mel Tillis

LuLu Roman

Mac Wiseman & Ronnie Reno

Mandy Barnett

Mark Chestnut

Mark Lowry

Mark Wills

Mickey Gilley

Williams & Ree

Mo Pitney & Bill Anderson

Neal McCoy

George Hamilton IV

Ray Stevens

Quebe Sisters

Ray Pillow

Rebecca Lynn Howard

Restless Heart

Charlie Daniels

Col. Littleton

John Berry

Roy Clark

Wilford Brimley

Buck Trent

Nadine

The Oak Ridge Boys & Johnny Lee

Jeannie Seely

Steve Hall & Shotgun Red

Sonny Curtis

Teea Goans

Sonny Osborne

T. Graham Brown

TG Sheppard

Tony Orlando

Tracy Lawrence

The Texas Tenors

The Whites

Wilson Fairchild

The Starlite THEATRE

Where the Stars Shine!

Sept 24-26: Gene Watson
417-337-9333
www.starlitetheatre.com

Travelin' Waitress

When I was a flying waitress (flight attendant) I did get to travel a lot. Each day we would board and deplane hundreds of folks with interesting stories. I really enjoyed working what we called "turns." Turns are quick flights. You would fly to a city, deplane, reboard and then return back to that same city. Sometimes I would do several turns in a day, and the challenge of doing turns was figuring out which city you were in for the onboard announcements. Since I rarely got off the plane between turns, I would literally have to look out the window to see where we were. And if you ask me what town or mountain range was below the aircraft, forget it.

This is very much like our Diner tapings. In the first few seasons, we taped all 13 episodes in a week. Since we don't ever stop tape except for a short break between shows, it would really get confusing. I would see pie sitting in the kitchen area and think, "Wow. Why do I have so much pie left?" and then remember, "Oh! This is a new show with new folks in the Diner, and they need food!"

There are many who would accidentally be served two of the same thing. Yep! I hate to admit it, but there is no rhyme or reason to who gets served what. If a customer eats fast (being the excellent waitress I am) I might grab his plate, clean the table, and by the third segment serve them another plate of food.

Larry would even forget to mention stuff on the show, thinking he had already mentioned it. So if you ever wondered if he "really" forgets to read the promise, the answer is YES!

A few years ago we changed our schedule. Now we tape our shows four times a year, 6-7 episodes in two days. We have a diner full of new guests for each show. We still forget stuff. We have even more folks coming to our tapings, so I am busier than ever. We are still a mess at times.

To add more interest to my life as a TV waitress, we have taken our Larry's Country Diner TV show on the road to the Starlite Theater in Branson, Mo. During one of our six weeks of performing, Larry had the sides of our bus wrapped with all of our photos. I don't know if anyone knew who we were or cared, but it sure made fun traveling. During our stage show, we actually recreate the Diner setting. I have six tables and about 24 chairs, and we invite folks from the audience to join us on stage. Although I can't serve hot food during our stage shows, I do serve coffee and pie (just like I do on our TV show.) If you haven't experienced one of our stage shows, you MUST! The cameras aren't rollin', but we still don't care and we still have lots of fun.

Bus

Diner in Branson

Diner on Cruise

Diner Lingo Quiz

What does it mean to "drown the kids?"

a. Pour milk over ice cream
b. Pour milk over cereal
c. Boil your eggs
d. Add chocolate sauce

Answer: Chap 11

71

Diner Lingo Quiz

What would be the best way to eat "elephant dandruff?"
a. In a bowl
b. On a stick
c. Sprinkled on ice cream
d. Spread on toast

Answer: Chap 11

72

My favorite thing every year is being a waitress on board our Cruises. We take approximately 1200 fans on a Country's Family Reunion and Larry's Country Diner Caribbean Cruise typically with nine country music legends.

Our Diner stage set is the same one we use in Branson. We have fans on stage with us, though it can be a little tricky serving HOT COFFEE with the ship moving. I am proud to say I haven't yet spilled any coffee or dropped any pie. Spending a week with our TV fans is the best experience ever. By the end of the Cruise everyone feels like family.

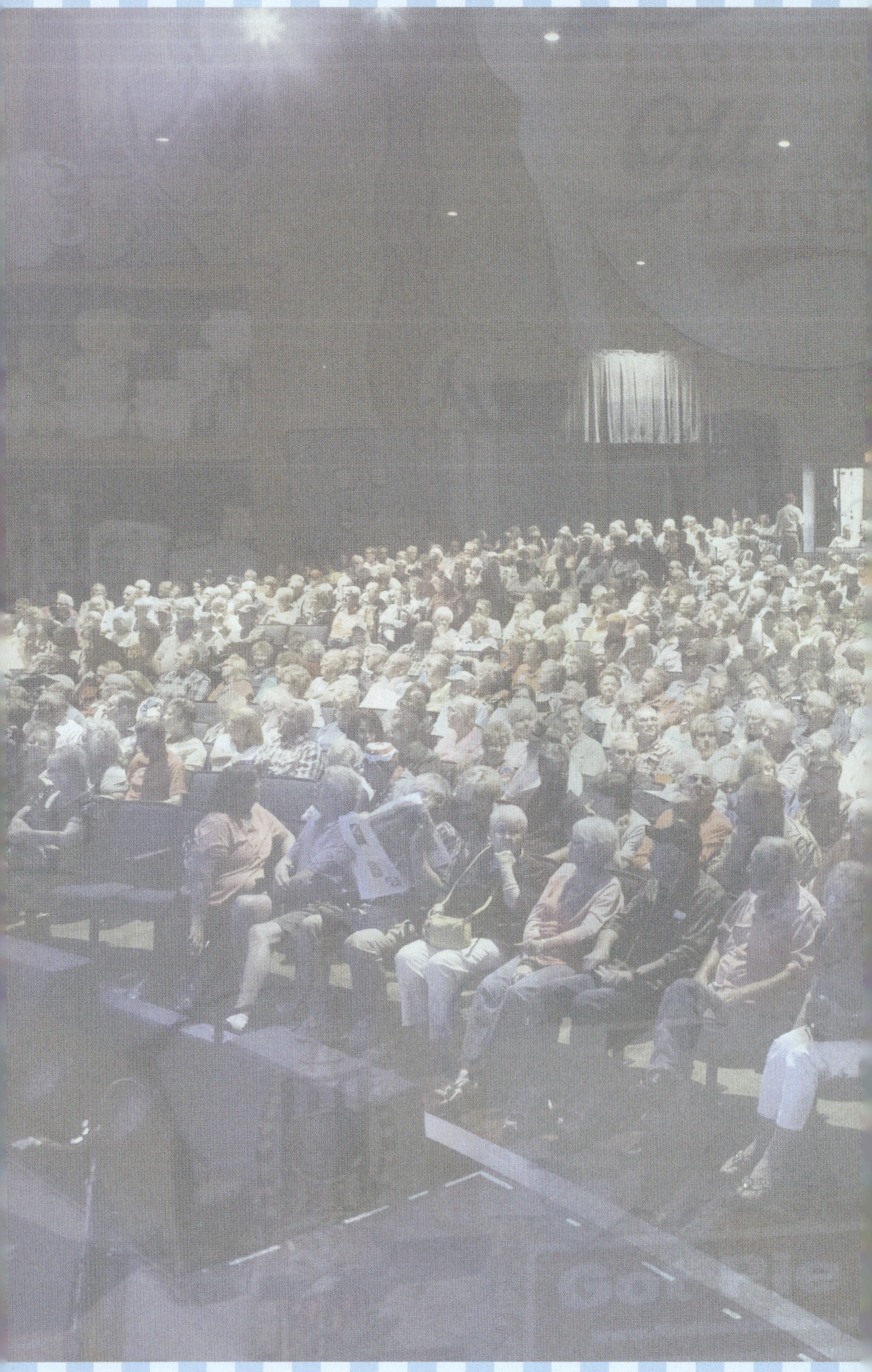

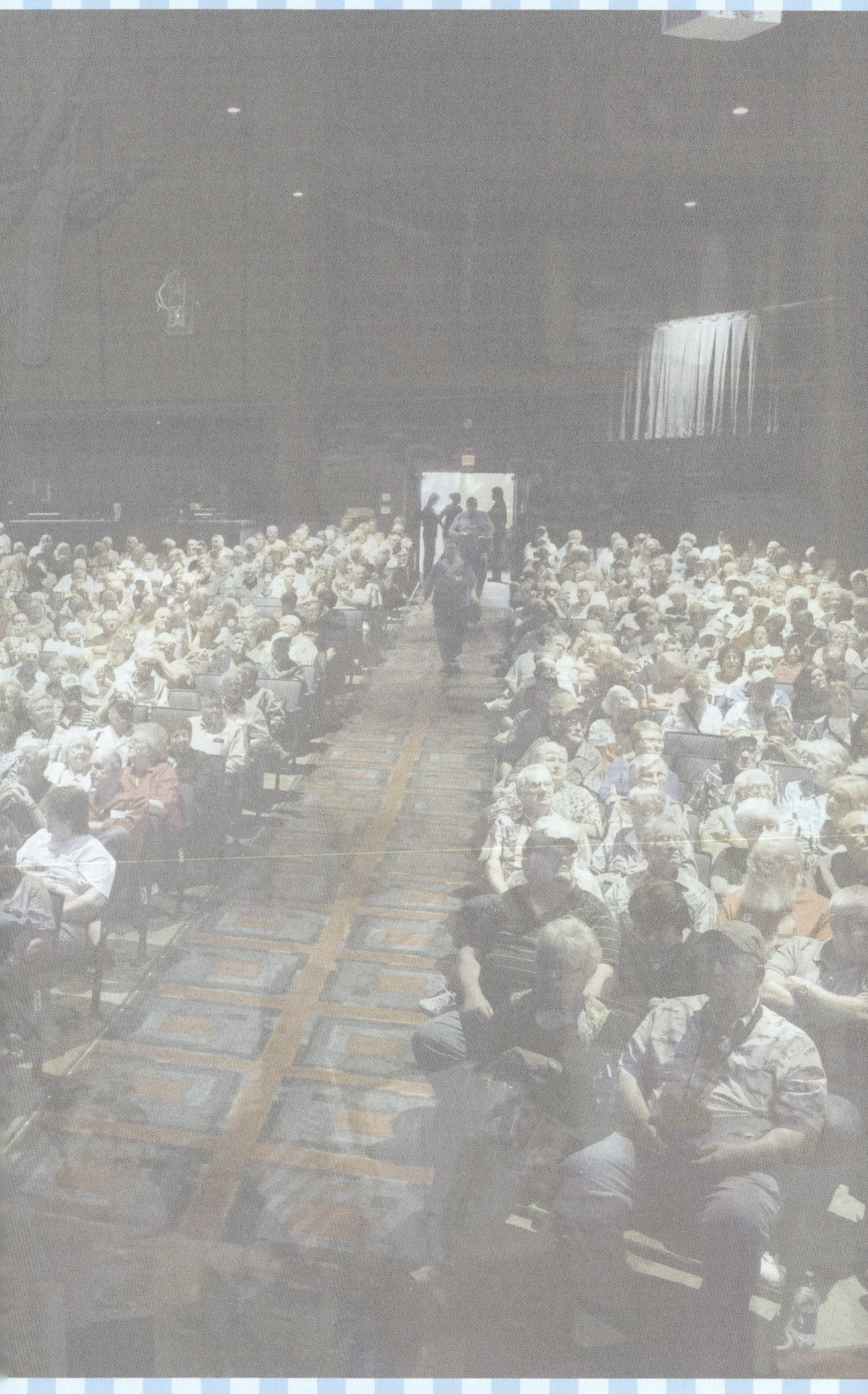

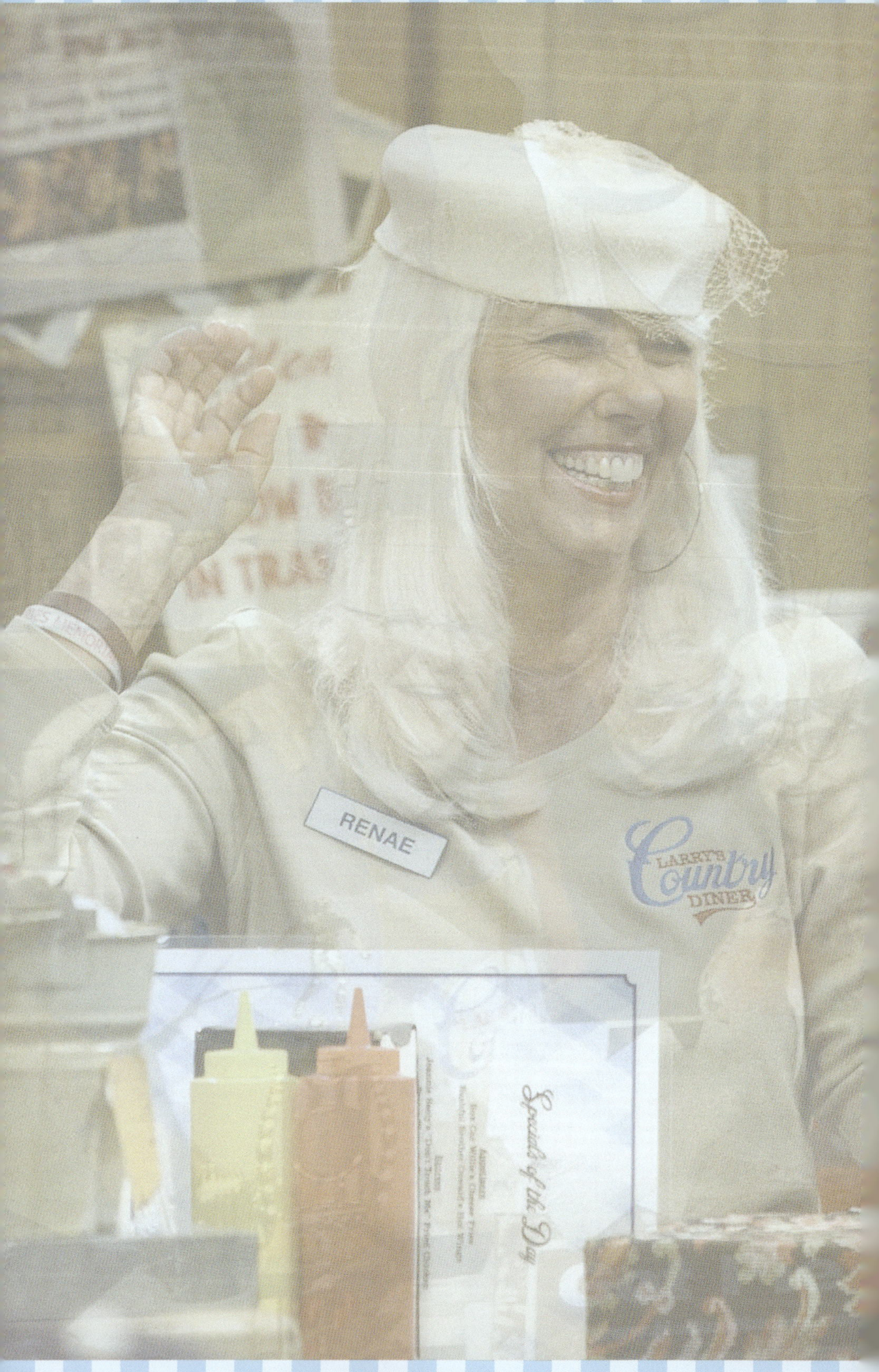
RENAE
LARRY'S Country DINER
Specials of the Day

10

Mind Your Manners

There are a lot of food establishments that are not very kid friendly. From the seating arrangements to the menu, you feel like there should be a sign hanging up that says "ADULT DINING ONLY." As a TV waitress, I have to admit I am excited to see those younger faces visit us on set. There are a lot more distractions to keep kids entertained than in a regular eating establishment, and of course no menu challenges.

However, there are some simple diner suggestions for eating out with kids. They not only make the mealtime pleasant but also keep the waitress from pulling her hair out.

1. Never arrive with starving kids. How can they be on their best behavior if they are already miserable? For heaven's sake, give them a snack before you arrive. A few crackers could make the wait time seem a lot shorter.

2. Determine what the kids are going to eat before you arrive. Are they finicky eaters? Do they have diet restrictions? If you want to teach them how to make decisions, talk it over before you arrive or sit down at the table.

3. Small kids talk rather loudly. Communicate with your child or children about the food choices and seating arrangements before sitting down. Teach them to use INSIDE voices. If they are with other children, make a game out of it.

4. Order one item for the kids ONLY to share. This can be fun and make kids feel special. If a child gets fidgety, take him on a short walk or visit the restroom. Restrooms are amazing. They have mirrors, water and paper towels (to draw on).

5. Small kids are well known for their short attention span. My favorite suggestion is to make a trip to the Dollar Store and buy something special for eating out. It could be an animal bib, a toy, a game, or coloring book--anything fun. Save it just for dining out.

6. Always have a light jacket or sweatshirt in the car. Diners can be chilly even in the summer months (with the air conditioner blowing).

7. Turn your cell phone off during dining times and teach your kids table manners, to say "Please" and "Thank you." Being rude to your waitress is never an option.

8. Do you say a blessing before you eat? A simple prayer could create a great habit and can also be fun for kids. Here is one that is easy to recite:

*God is great, God is good,
let us thank him for our food. AMEN.*

Diner Lingo Quiz

Which of these is "not" a way to ask for butter in diner lingo?

a. Axle grease
b. Cow to cover
c. Cow paste
d. Sweet Alice

Answer: Chap 11

79

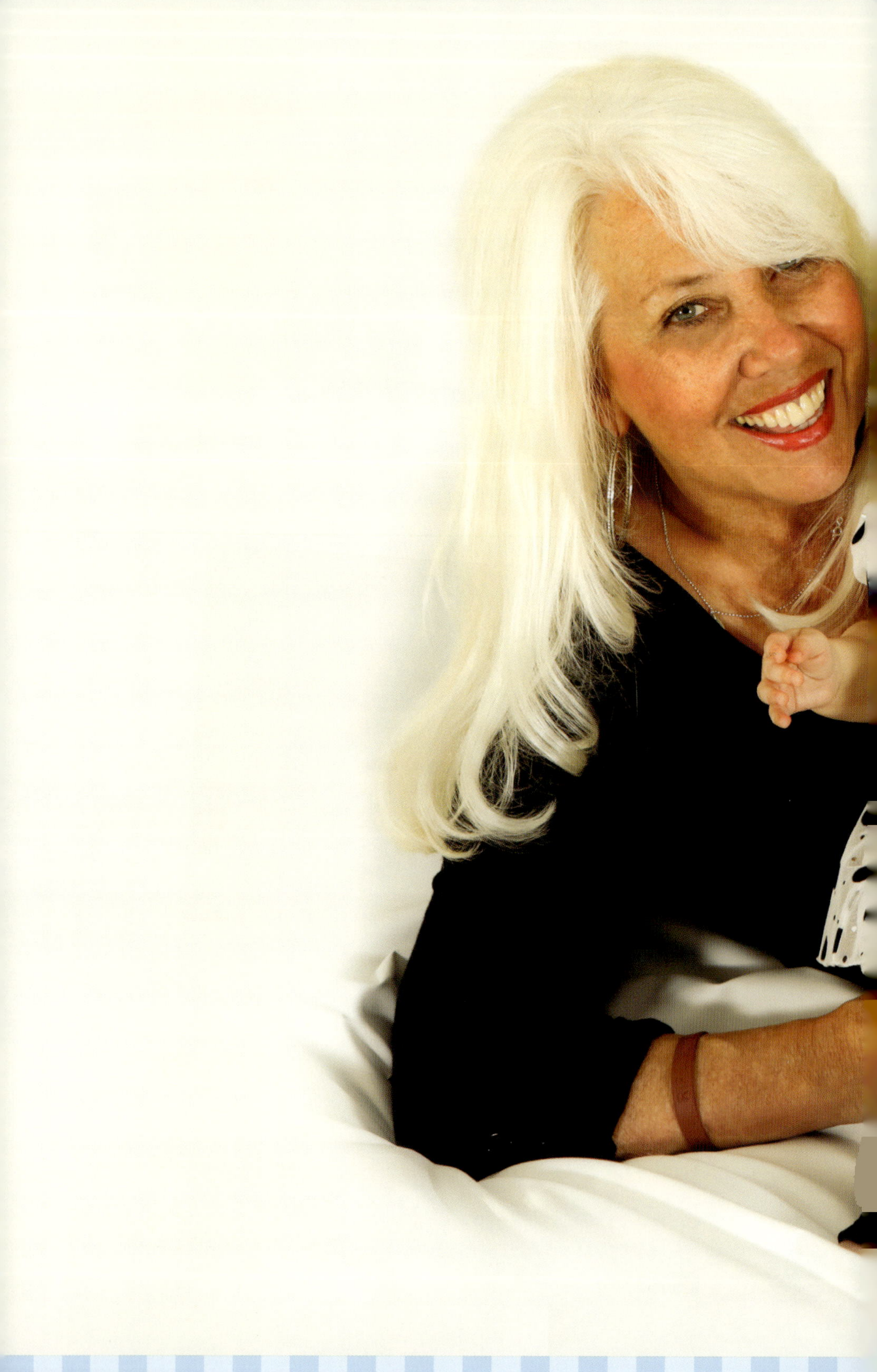

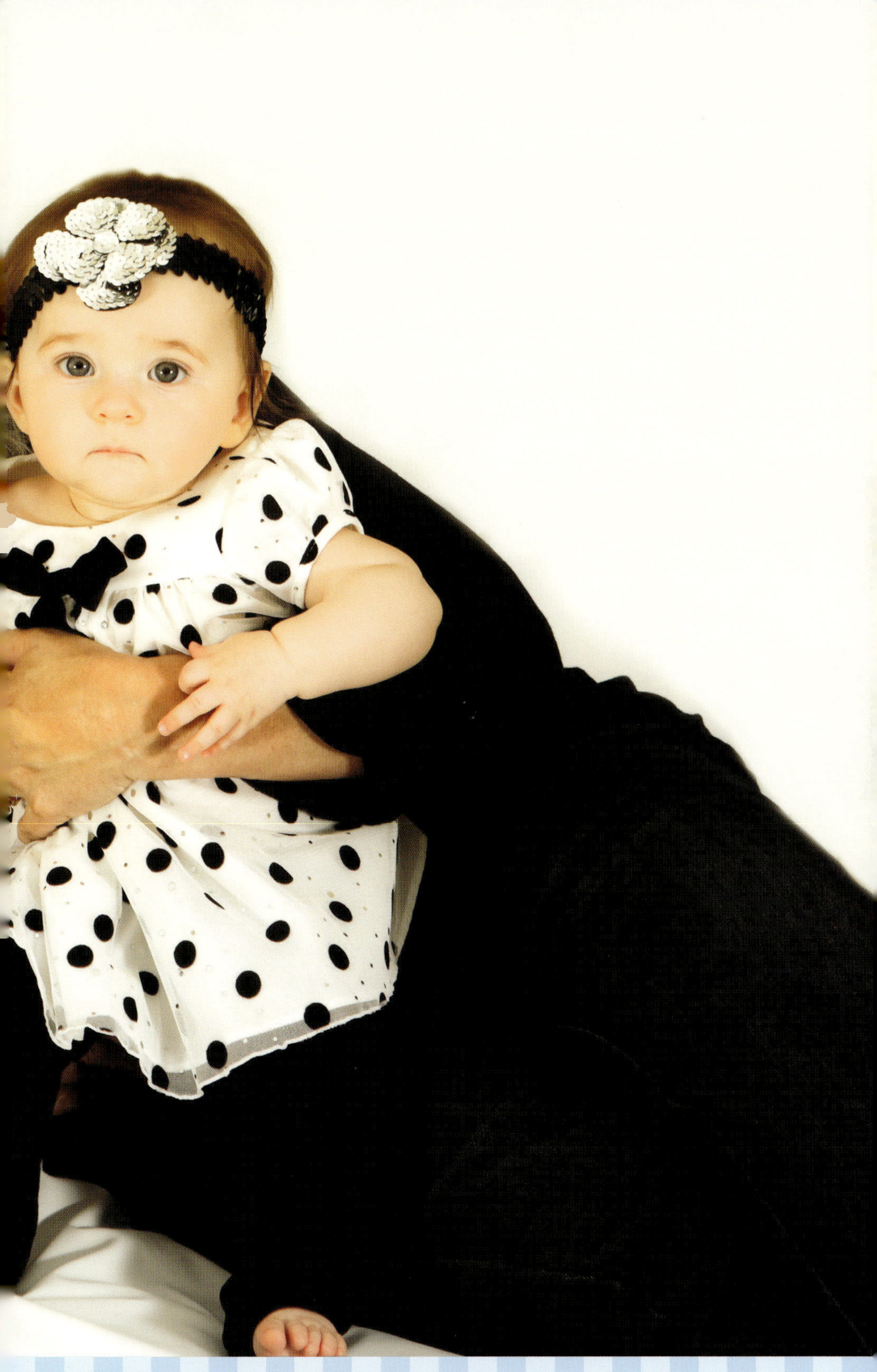

9. Teach kids to chew with their mouths closed and use a napkin. Teach them to sit up straight and not place their arms and elbows on the table.

10. Teach them to take a compliment. Wow. That is something ADULTS don't know how to do! So learn yourself while you teach your kids.

11. Teach kids where to place their fork, spoon and knife. That can be a fun game.

12. Bribe kids to encourage good behavior and have consequences for bad behavior.

But, remember, consequences should not be given for something the parents have not taught.

AND PARENTS, don't drink when you take your kids out with you and remember to TIP your waitress! This is the time to BLESS someone that is serving you. Teach your children to give with a giving heart.

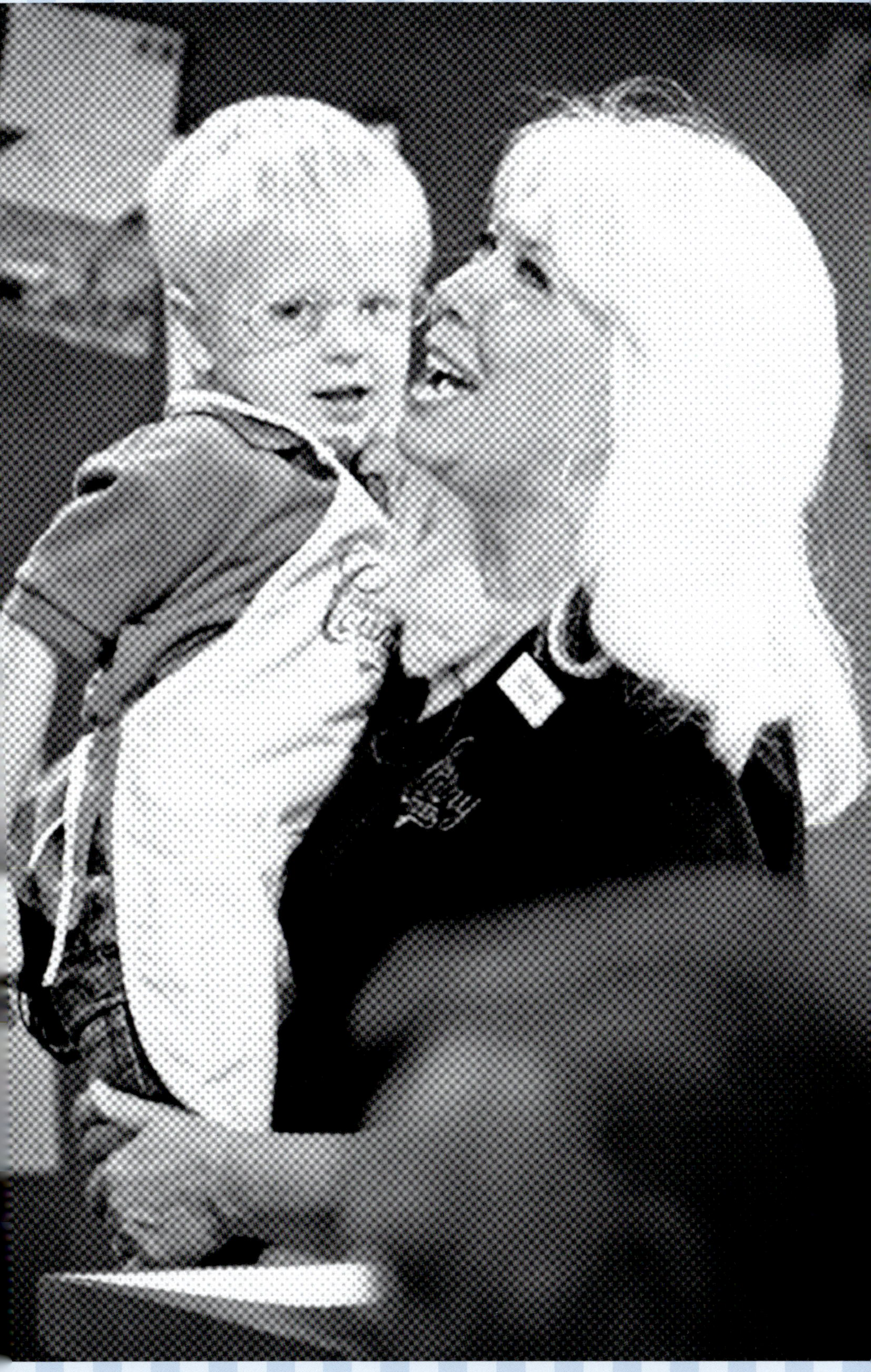

SAM BAM

Serving kids at our Diner tapings is fun. I especially look forward to the times when Larry's grandkids show up. Sam Bam, of course, has been on our show the most and everyone seems to know him. He is the spitting image of his Papa Larry, especially all dressed up in his Diner shirt, carrying his red towel and wearing his look-alike glasses. Larry loves to ask him questions just to see what he says, which is really not any different from what he does to adults on the show.

> *"I especially look forward to the times when Larry's grandkids show up."*

Larry has ten grandkids, so when I became a grandmother I had to bring my little granddaughter to the Diner for everyone to meet. Rio was born on August 16, 2013, and she is the cherry on my sundae!

TV Diner Lingo

The origin of Diner lingo is unknown but there is evidence that it was used in the United States as early as the 1870's . Many of the terms might be considered politically incorrect these days but were used as lighthearted and tongue-in-cheek for short-order cooks and staff. Diner Lingo was most popular in diners and luncheonettes from 1920s to 1970s. There can be variations of the meanings depending on what part of the country you are in and what type of diner.

If you have watched our TV show, Larry's Country Diner, you have seen Keith throw some Diner Lingo at me. These slang phrases and meanings can be really fun and a challenge. I have put together some of my favorite diner lingo along with quiz questions through out my book I hope these terms stir some memories and bring a smile next time you visit a diner.

Diner Quiz Answers: p.9: b / p.12: c / p.16: a / p.28: c / p.38: c
p.40: d / p.47: d / p.50: d / p.57: a / p.66: b
p.73: c / p.74: a / p.81: d

A

A-pie — Apple pie

Abbott and Costello — Franks and beans

Acid — Vinegar

Adam and Eve on a log — Two poached eggs and a sausage link

Adam and Eve on a raft — Two poached eggs on toast

Adam and Eve on a raft, and wreck 'em — Two scrambled eggs on toast

Adam's ale — Water

Adam's ale, hold the hail — Water with no ice

Aggies — Baked beans

Alive — Raw more...

All arms and legs — Weak

All black — Chocolate soda with chocolate ice cream

All hot — Baked potato

All the way — Served with all the toppings For a burger, this usually means "with lettuce, mayonnaise, onion, and butter." This phrase may also refer to chocolate cake with chocolate ice cream.

Alleviator — Glass of tomato juice with black coffee

Angel food cake and wine — Bread and water

Angels on horseback — Oysters rolled in bacon and served on toast

Ant paste — Chocolate pudding

Arches — Eggs

Arizona — Buttermilk

Athlete's foot — Stewed, dried peaches

Atlanta special — Coca-Cola more...

Axle grease — Butter

B

B and B — Bread and butter

B.L.T. — Bacon, lettuce, and tomato sandwich.

Baby — Glass of milk

Baby juice — Milk

Baby sauce — Mustard

Back teeth afloat — Intoxicated

Bad breath — Onion

Baked Alaska — Baked Swiss steak

Bald headed row — Row of diner seats

Baled hay — Shredded wheat

Ball of fire — Shot of whiskey

Balloon juice — Seltzer or soda water

Balloon water — Seltzer or soda water

Bang berries — Baked beans

Bank — Cash register

Bark — Hot dog

Barked pie — Fruit cobbler

Barley broth — Beer

Barley water — Beer

Barn stormer — Waitress who jumps from job-to-job

Base runner — Waitress who jumps from job-to-job

Battery acid — Grapefruit juice

Beadsteader — Sleepy counterman

Bean buster — Heavy eater

Beans to go — Coffee

Beef a la mode — Beef stew

Beef-on-wreck — Famous style of roast beef sandwich

Beef stick — Bone

Bees — American cheese

Beetle blood — Beer (usually ale)

Belch water — Seltzer or soda water

Belly busters — Baked beans

Belly cheat — Apron

Belly chokers — Doughnuts

Belly furniture — Food

Belly warmer — Cup of coffee

Bellywash — Soup

Bend the crab — To overcharge a rude customer

Bender — An employee who steals food

Bernice — Aspirin or other pain-killers

Berries — Eggs

Bessie — Roast beef or hamburger

Bib — Napkin

Bible — Cook book

Biddy board — French toast

Billiard — Buttermilk

Bing — Small restaurant

Birdseed — Breakfast cereal

Biscuit — Your heart

Biscuit grabber — Fatty food

Black and blue — Extremely rare meat.

Black and white — Chocolate soda with vanilla ice cream

Black ball — Chocolate ice cream

Black bottom — Chocolate ice cream with chocolate syrup

Black box — Safe or cash register

Black cow — Chocolate milk or milkshake

Black stick — Chocolate ice cream cone

Black water — Root beer

Blindfolded — Basted eggs

Blonde — Coffee with cream

Blonde and sweet — Coffee with cream and sugar

Blonde with sand — Coffee with cream and sugar

Bloodhound — Hot dog

Bloodhound in the hay — Hot dog with sauerkraut

Bloody — Very rare

Blowout patches — Pancakes

Blue-bottle — Bromo Seltzer

Blue-plate special — A daily special of meat, potatoes and a vegetable

Boiled leaves — Hot tea

Bossy in a bowl — Beef stew

Bossy on a board — Roast beef sandwich

Bottom — Scoop of ice cream added to a drink

Bow-wow — Hot dog

Bowl of red — Chili soup

Bowl on fire — Chili soup

Break it and shake it — To add an egg to a drink

Breath — Onion

Bridge party — Four of something

Broken hen berries — Scrambled eggs

Bronx vanilla — Garlic

Brown bellies — Baked beans

Brown down — Wheat toast

Bubble dancer — Dishwasher

Bucket of cold mud — Bowl of chocolate ice cream

Bucket of hail — Glass of ice

Bullets — Baked beans

Bun pup — Hot dog

Burger with breath — Hamburger with onions

Burn one — Put a hamburger on the grill

Burn one, take it through the garden and pin a rose on it — Hamburger with lettuce, tomato, and onion

Burn the British — Toasted English muffin

Butcher's revenge — Meatloaf

C

C.B. — Cheeseburger

C.J. Boston — Cream cheese and jelly sandwich

C.J. white — Cream cheese and jelly sandwich on white bread

Cackle fruit — Eggs

Cackleberries — Eggs

Canary Island special — Vanilla soda with chocolate ice cream

Canned cow — Evaporated milk

Cat's eyes — Tapioca pudding

Check the ice — Look at the attractive girl who just came in

Checkerboard — Waffle

Chewed with fine breath — Hamburger with onions

Chicago dog — Steamed bun with relish

Chicago sundae — Pineapple sundae more...

Chicken in the hay — Egg salad sandwich

Chicks on a raft — Eggs on toast

China — Rice pudding

Choker hole — Doughnut

Chokies — Artichokes

Chopper — Knife

City juice — Water

Clean up the kitchen — Order of hash

Cluck — Eggs

Cluck and grunt — Eggs and bacon

Coke pie — Coconut pie

Cold mud — Chocolate ice cream

Cold spot — Iced tea

Coney Island — Hot dog

Corrugated roof — Lemon meringue pie

Corsage — With onions

Cow feed — Salad

Cow juice — Milk

Cow paste — Butter

Cow to cover — Butter

Cowboy — Western omelette

Cowboy coffee — Coffee from chicory beans

Cowboy with spurs — Western omelette with french fries

Creep — Draft beer

Cremate — To burn (or toast) something

Crowd — Three of something

Cup of mud — Coffee

Customer will take a chance — Order of hash

Cut the grass — Serve without relish

D

Dagwood special — Banana split

Deadeye — Poached egg

Devils on horseback — Prunes rolled in bacon, served on toast

Dine and dash — Leaving without paying the bill

Dirty water — Coffee

Dog and maggot — Cracker and cheese

Dog biscuit — Cracker

Dog soup — Water

Double black cow — Extra rich chocolate shake

Dough well done — Toast

Dough well done with cow to cover — Buttered toast

Douse it — Cover it in sauce

Drag one through Georgia — Cola with chocolate syrup

Drag one through the garden — Put all the condiments on it

Drag one through Wisconsin — Put cheese on it

Draw one — Cup of coffee

Draw one in the dark — Cup of black coffee

Draw one muddy — Cup of black coffee

Drop two — Two poached eggs

Drown one, hold the hail — Coca Cola with no ice

Drown the kids — Boil the eggs

Dry — Plain, no condiments

Dry stack — Pancakes with no butter or syrup

Dusty miller — Chocolate pudding sprinkled with powdered malt

E

Easy over — Eggs briefly cooked and flipped

Echo — Repeat the order

Egg cream — Drink made with chocolate syrup, milk, and seltzer

Eighty-one — Glass of water

Eighty-six — Cancel the order

Elephant dandruff — Corn flakes cereal

English winter — Iced tea

Eternal twins — Ham and eggs

Eve with a lid on — Apple pie

Eve with a moldy lid — Apple pie with a slice of cheese

F

Family reunion — Chicken and egg sandwich

Fifty-five — Glass of root beer

Fifty-one — Hot chocolate

First lady — An order of ribs

Fish eyes — Tapioca pudding

Five — Glass of milk

Flat car — Pork chops

Flop two — Two fried eggs

Flop two, over easy — Two fried eggs, flipped over with a runny yolk

Flop two, over hard — Two fried eggs, flipped over with a solid yolk

Flop two, over medium — Two fried eggs, flipped over with a creamy yoke

Florida tonic — Orange juice

Flowing Mississippi — Coffee

Fly cake — Raisin cake

Fog — Mashed potatoes

Foreign entanglements — Spaghetti

Forty-one — Lemonade

Forty-two — Two orders of eggs flipped over

Frenchman's delight — Pea soup

Friday's choice — Fish dinner

Frog sticks — French fries

Frosty joe — Iced coffee

Fry two, let the sun shine — Two fried eggs with unbroken yolks

Full house — Grilled cheese sandwich with bacon and tomato

G

GAC — Grilled American cheese sandwich

Gallery — Diner booth

Gentlemen will take a chance — Order of hash

George Eddy — A customer who doesn't leave tips

Georgia pie — Peach pie

Give it shoes — Make it a take-out order

Go for a walk — Make it a take-out order

Gravel train — Sugar bowl

Graveyard stew — Buttered toast with sugar and cinnamon, served in a bowl of warm milk

Groundhog — Hot dog

Grunt — Bacon

H

Hail — Ice

Halitosis — Garlic

Hamlette — Omelette made with ham

Harlem midget — Small chocolate soda

Harlem soda — Chocolate soda

Heart attack on rack — Biscuits and gravy

Hemorrhage — Ketchup

Hen berries — Eggs

High and dry — A sandwich without condiments

High, yellow, black and white — Chocolate soda with vanilla ice cream

Hoboken special — Pineapple soda with chocolate ice cream

Hockey puck — Well-done hamburger

Hold the grass — No lettuce

Hold the hail — No ice

Honeymoon salad — Salad with just lettuce

Hope — Oatmeal

Hops — Malted milk powder

Hot balls — Matzoh ball soup

Hot blonde in the sand — Coffee with cream and sugar

Hot cha — Hot chocolate

Hot one — Bowl of chili soup

Hot spot — Tea or coffee

Hot top — Hot chocolate

Hounds on an island — Franks and beans

Houseboat — Banana split

Hug one — Glass of orange juice

I

Ice on rice — Rice pudding with ice cream

Idaho cakes — Hash brown patties

In a fog — Served with mashed potatoes

In the alley — Served as a side dish

In the hay — Strawberry milkshake

Irish turkey — Corned beef and cabbage

Italian perfume — Garlic

J

Jack — Grilled American cheese sandwich

Jack Benny — Grilled cheese with bacon

Jack Benny in the Red — Strawberry Jell-O

Jack Tommy — Grilled cheese with tomato

Java — Coffee

Jayne Mansfield — Tall stack of pancakes

Jerk — Ice cream soda

Joe — Coffee

Joe O'Malley — Irish coffee

K

Kansas dog — Hot dog with mustard and cheese

Keep off the grass — No lettuce

Kiss the pan — Eggs over easy

L

L.A. — Serve it with ice cream

Ladybug — Fountain operator

Late walk — A take-out order

Leaves in the hail — Iced tea

Let it swim — Ice cream floated on top

Let it walk — Make it a take-out order

Let the sun shine — Don't break the yokes

Life preservers — Doughnuts

Lighthouse — Bottle of ketchup

Log roll — Order of link sausages

Looseners — Prunes

Lord's supper — Bread and water

Love apples — Tomatoes

Lumber — A toothpick

M

M.D. — Dr. Pepper

Magoo — Custard pie

Maiden's delight — Cherries

Make it a virtue — Add cherry syrup to a soda

Make it crackle — Add an egg to a drink, especially milkshakes

Make it cry — Add onions

Make it moo — Add milk to a coffee

Make it walk — Make it a take-out order

Mama — Marmalade

Mama on a raft — Marmalade on toast

Mayo — Mayonnaise

Melting snow — Melted Swiss cheese

Mickey Rooney — Served with mustard and relish

Mike and Ike — Salt and pepper shakers

Million on a platter — Order of baked beans

Mississippi mud — Mustard

Moo juice — Milk

Motor oil — Syrup

Mud — Black coffee

Mud of murk — Black coffee

Mully — Beef stew

Murphy — Potato

Mystery in the alley — Side order of hash

N

Nervous pudding — Bowl of Jell-O

No cow — Without milk

Noah's boy — Slice of ham

Noah's boy on bread — Ham sandwich

Noah's boy with Murphy carrying a wreath — Ham and potatoes with cabbage

Nun's toast — Hard-boiled eggs and flour gravy poured over toast

O

O.J. — Orange juice

Oh gee — Orange juice

Old maids — Prunes

On the hoof — Cooked rare

On wheels — Make it a take-out order

One from the Alps — Swiss cheese sandwich

One on the city — Glass of water

P

P.C. — Plain chocolate milk

P.T. — Pot of tea

Paint a bow-wow red — Hot dog with ketchup

Paint it red — Put ketchup on it

Pair of drawers — Two cups of coffee

Pig in a blanket — Ham sandwich

Pigs — Strips of bacon

Pigs between the sheets — Ham sandwich

Pin a rose on it — Add onion to it

Pink stick — Strawberry ice cream

Pipes — Straws

Pittsburgh — To toast or burn something

Pittsburgh rare — Burnt on the outside, rare on the inside

Plain and dry — Without any condiments

Pope Benedict — Eggs benedict

Popeye — Spinach

Put a hat on it — Add ice cream

Put legs on it — Make it a take-out order

Put out the lights and cry — Liver and onions

Q

Quail — Hungarian Goulash

R

Rabbit food — Lettuce

Radar range — Microwave oven

Radio sandwich — Tuna fish sandwich

Raft — Toast

Red and white — Topped with sour cream and salsa

Roach cake — Raisin cake

Rubber in a bun — Steak sandwich

Ruff it — Add whipped cream

Run it through the garden — Add all the condiments

S

Saddle it — Well-done steak

Sand — Sugar

Saturday nights — Baked beans

Scrape two — Two scrambled eggs

Sea dust — Salt

Shake it — Milkshake

Shake one in the hay — Strawberry milkshake

Shingle with a shimmy and a shake — Buttered toast with jam

Shit on a shingle — Chipped beef with gravy on toast

Shivering Eve — Apple jelly

Shivering hay — Strawberry Jell-O

Shivering Liz — Jell-O

Shoot it yellow — Add lemon syrup to a cola

Shoot one from the south — Make a cola extra strong

Short stack — Order of pancakes

Side arms — Salt and pepper

Side of Joan of Arc — French fries

Sinkers — Doughnuts

Sinkers and suds — Doughnuts and coffee

Skid grease — Butter

Slab of moo, let him chew it — Rare round steak

Sleigh ride special — Vanilla pudding

Small stretch — Small Coca-Cola

Smear — Butter

Sneeze — Pepper

Snowball — Scoop of vanilla ice cream

Soda — Carbonated water, usually flavored and colored

Soda jerk — Soda fountain worker

Soup jockey — Waitress

Sour it — Add lemon to it

Spike on an oval — Order of hash browns

Splash from the garden — Bowl of vegetable soup

Splash of red noise — Bowl of tomato soup

Spot with a twist — Cup of tea with lemon

Squeeze one — Glass of orange juice

St. Pats — Corned beef and cabbage

Stack — Order of pancakes

Stack of Vermont — Pancakes with syrup

Steaming Idaho — Baked potato

Still mooing — Served rare

Stretch one — Coca-cola

Stretch one and paint it red — Coca-Cola with cherry syrup

Submarine — Doughnut

Suds — Beer

Sun kiss — Orange juice

Sunny brook — Eggs fried without flipping with bacon

Sunny side up — Fried eggs without breaking the yolks

Sunny sundae — Ice cream sundae with **pineapple**

Suthun coffee — Half regular beans, and half chicory

Swamp water — Soda made with all flavors available

Sweep the kitchen — Order of hash

Sweet Alice — Milk

T

Take a chance — Order of hash

Take it to the garden — Add lettuce, tomato and onion

A thousand on a plate — Baked beans

Throw it in the mud — Add chocolate syrup

Tip toe through Wisconsin — Sprinkle cheese on it

Top it red — Add salsa

Top it white — Add sour cream

Tube steak — Hot dog

Tuna down — Tuna fish sandwich

Twelve alive — A dozen raw oysters

Twenty-one — Limeade

The twins — Salt and pepper shakers

Twist it, choke it, and make it cackle — Chocolate malt with egg

Two cows, make 'em cry — Two hamburgers with onions

Two dots and a dash — Two fried eggs and a strip of bacon

V

Velvet — Milkshake

Vermont — Maple syrup

Virgin Mary — Bloody Mary with no alcohol

Virtue — Cherry pie

W

Walk a cow through the garden — Burger with lettuce, tomato and onion

Warts — Olives

Wax — American cheese

Wheat down — Toasted wheat bread

Whiskey down — Toasted rye bread

Whistle berries — Baked beans

White cow — Vanilla milkshake

Wimpy — Hamburger

Winter — Whipped cream

With legs — Make it a take-out order

With the horns on — Served rare

The works — All the condiments

Wreath — Cabbage

Wreck 'em — Scrambled eggs

Wrecked and crying — Scrambled eggs with onions

Wrecked hen with fruit — Scrambled eggs and orange juice

Y

Yellow paint — Mustard

Yum-yum — Sugar

Z

Z — Mushrooms

Zeppelin — Sausage

Zeppelins in a fog — Sausages and mashed potatoes

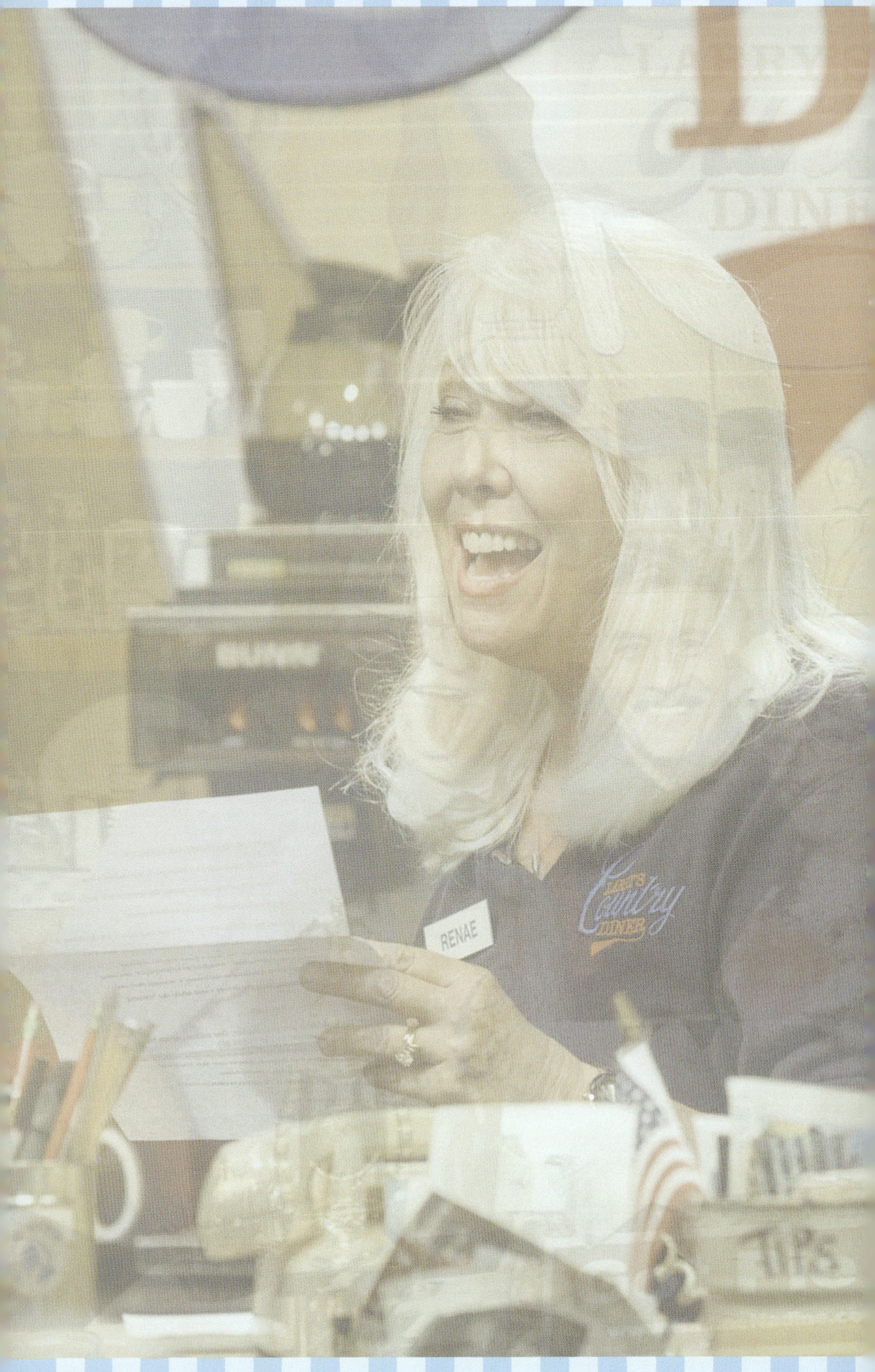
RENAE
TIPS

12

Ask Your Waitress

Have you ever thought about what your Waitress hears?? She is at your table many times filling up your drink, removing your plates, and checking to see what you need. She may not speak or interrupt your conversation but she is there ... listening and hearing some of the most intimate conversations. As a TV waitress there is not much conversation at the tables I wait on. Most customers are aware that I wear a microphone and cameras are everywhere. However there are questions that I am ask over and over through mail, over the phone and at our stage shows. So I would like to answer some of those questions for you.

1. Am I related to Larry Black?

I am not related to Larry nor am I married to Larry. Even though his wife, Luann refers to me as his TV wife. I started working for Larry in 1998 when he started Country's Family Reunion. I am actually VP of Operations for our corporate offices at Gabriel Communications/Country's Family Reunion. My office is next to Larry's office and yes...he does yell "Renae" a lot.

2. Do I serve real food?

Yes. During our show tapings we have a make shift kitchen with a great staff who prepares all the food. They actually cook it during the show and have it ready for me to bring through the swinging door. Since Springer Mountain Farms Chicken became our sponsor we are now serving Chicken with cold slaw and yummy pie.

3. Is Nadine a man?

No. Do you really think Larry would have a cross-dresser on the show? Nadine is a very attractive woman. Her husband is an Optometrist and she works full time as his assistant. Nadine was born in 1951 ... you figure it out. She does write her own material.

4. What kind of guitar does the Sheriff play?

Jimmy usually plays a Blue Ridge guitar on the Diner shows. Model #BR143 CE. His amp is a Little Walter.

5. Is Jimmy Capps a real Sheriff?

No. Jimmy Capps is not in law enforcement. However, on one of the shows he was made an honorary Davidson County Sheriff. Jimmy is a Nashville session musician (picker) and was recently inducted into the Nashville Musicians Hall Of Fame. He has been apart of the Grand Ole Opry band since 1967.

6. Was I a real Private Investigator?

Yes. I was a store detective for several years at which time I applied for my PI License. I only worked for a short period of time undercover with a private company.

107

7. Is the Sheriff married to Michele?

Yes. Jimmy and Michele married July 15, 2007, twelve years after they first met.

8. How many years was Keith the announcer for the Grand Ole Opry?

From 1982-2009 . In addition he was the weatherman on The Ralph Emery show from 1976-2000.

9. Is Larry's Country Diner TV show in a real diner?

No. Our television shows are filmed at North Star Studios in Nashville Tennessee. You might be interested to know we also film our Country's Family Reunion shows there also.

10. Can I get tickets to Larry's Country Diner taping?

Yes. We usually tape our shows 4 times a year. Feb, June, August and December. We only have room for about 30 folks in the actual diner per show and we tape 6-7 shows in two days. Needless to say our tapings get booked up fairly quickly.

11. Is my hair real and is this my natural color?

Yes. It is my real hair and my color has evolved by getting gray prematurely. However as I tell anyone who asks, "Gray doesn't come in evenly." So I do add a product called Color Silk about every 6 weeks. This covers the dark patches that has not grayed.

12. Who am I married to?

I am married to Phil Johnson who is our staff photographer. Phil was a Dove Award & Gammy nominated Christian Record producer and song writer for over 30 years working with such Christian artists as Dottie Rambo, The Imperials, Evie Tornquist, Dallas Holm, The Martins, The Easters, Gloria Gaither, The Oak Ridge Boys, Gordon Mote to name a few. Phil was ask to sing one of his most popular Christian songs on our Country's Family Reunion " Old Time Gospel " titled "The Day He Wore My Crown". He also wrote and sang a cute little "Diner" song he performed on Larry's Country Diner titled "Renae, Renae ... I sure need some sugar today".

13. How is your Grandbaby?

Rio was born August 16, 2013 and a total joy!! I have had her visit the Diner several times and she loves it. I am not sure what she is going to call me but believe me I will answer to anything. Stay tuned to the Diner for more visits from Rio.

Justin

I would like to thank everyone who has asked about our son, Justin.

Justin was 28 years old when he was killed on News Years morning 2008 in an automobile accident on his way to work. Justin had recently received his college degree and was saving money to go to China and reunite with his fiancé and teach English. Losing a child is the most life changing experience that could ever happen to you. And only those who have lost a child would understand. So many of you have called and sent letters after hearing Phil sing on Country's Family Reunion "Old Time Gospel" series and the song he wrote sung by Gordon Mote "Hold Me Up". I want to thank you for your love and support and also sharing your loss. I pray we continue to hold each other up with a hug...a smile and a prayer as the Lord holds us up when we can't find our wings. We miss Justin everyday but we know he is safe in the arms of his heavenly father.

HOLD ME UP
Written By Phil Johnson

Lord, you promised there'd be nothing
That we couldn't make it through
And in my heart
I know Your Word is true
It's just these waters that I'm sailing through
Right now are mighty rough
Could you wrap me in Your arms
And hold me up?

Hold me up
So I can sing
I've been trying hard to fly
But I can't find my wings
I am traveling through a time
When all I have is not enough
I need to hear Your voice
And feel Your touch
Could you wrap me in Your arms
And hold me up?

Lord, I know I'm not the only one
Whose heart is hurting now
There are others, Lord,
Who need to feel Your power
If anyone knows how we feel,
Lord, we know it's You
So please come and do what only You can do

Hold us up
So we can sing
We've been trying hard to fly
But we can't find our wings
We are traveling through a time
When all we have is not enough
We need to hear Your voice
And feel Your touch
Could you wrap us in Your arms
And hold us up?

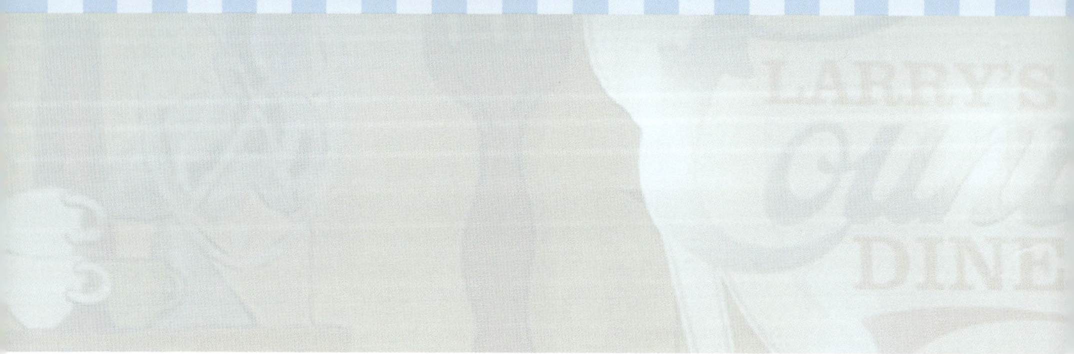

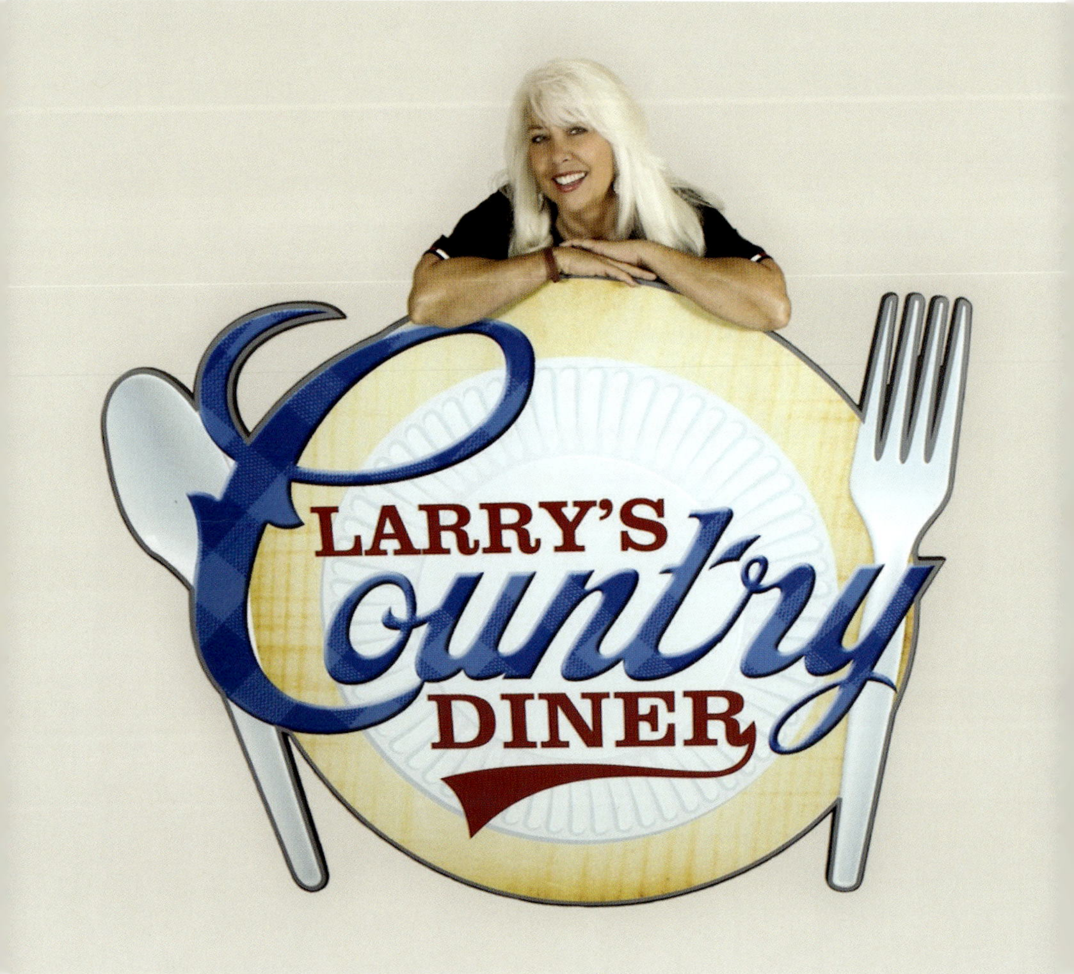
LARRY'S
Country
DINER

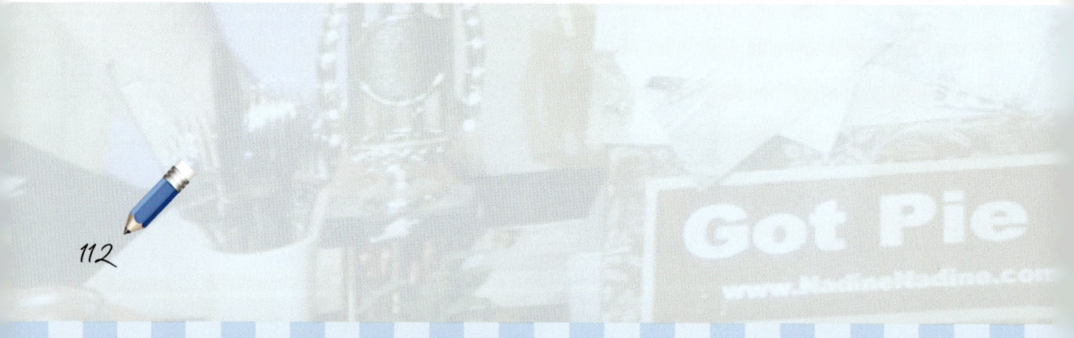
Got Pie

Reservations

Making a reservation at a country diner may seem unnecessary unless you want to visit *Larry's Country Diner*. Reservation can be the hottest ticket in town with a wait list of 2 years. We usually open our reservations once a year and it is filled within a few hours for the whole year with a wait list. Because we can only seat around 40-50 folks in the Diner including our sponsors, artist, guests and family it doesn't take long. However ... we do have cancelations from time to time.

I remember the first couple of shows we taped there were only a few people who actually showed up to sit in the diner. We removed some of the tables and chairs and filled the rest of the tables with family and friends and anyone else we could drag in. So you can imagine our surprise when we started getting emails and phone calls from people asking where the Diner was located and could they come. We realized that viewers from our television show thought we were an actual "diner" and yep ... I was a real waitress. By our second season we had added tables and chairs back to our set so we could accommodate more folks. And it wasn't long before our reservations were full and the only problem we had was finding enough space. And space can be a major problem for me.

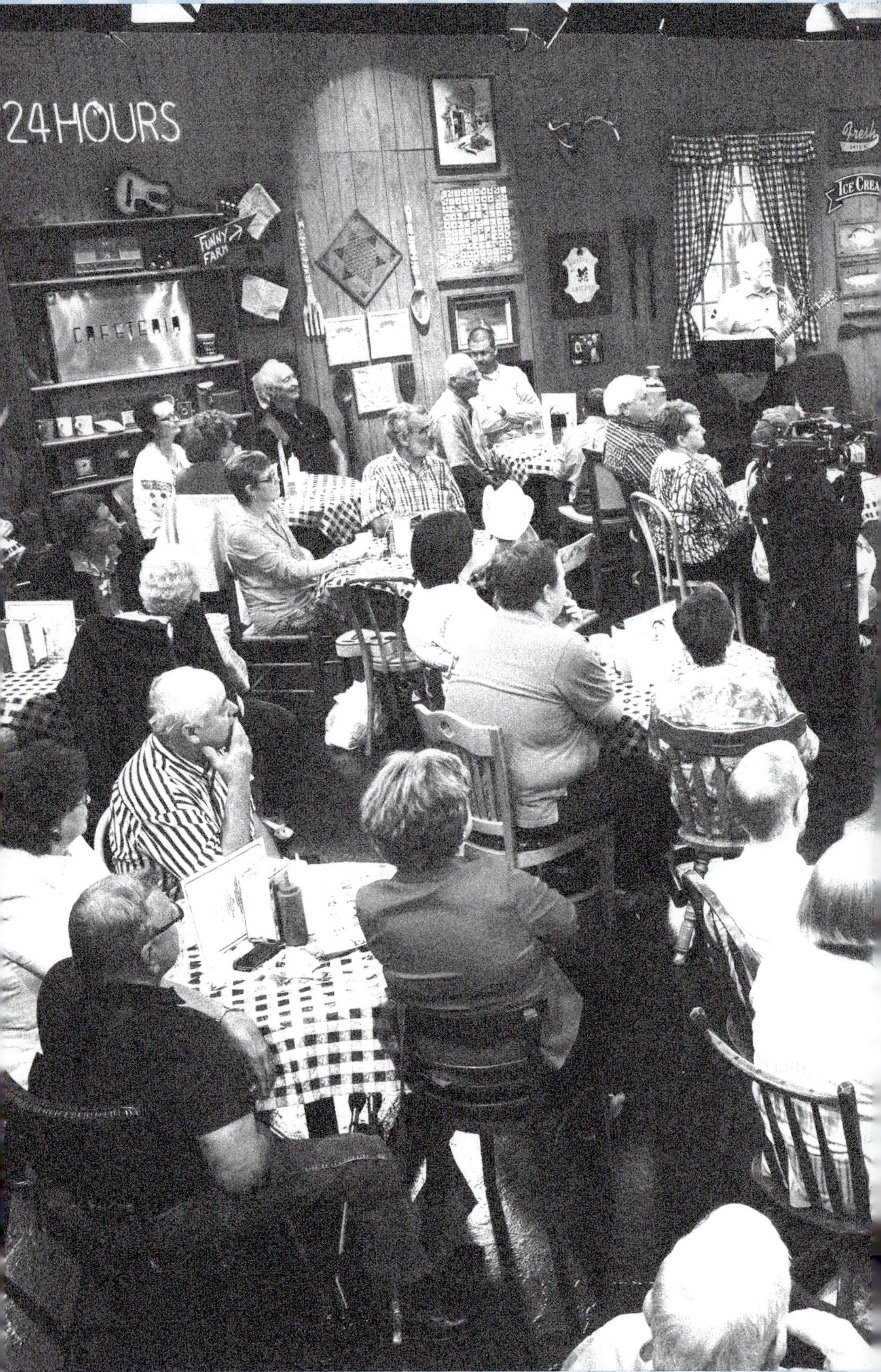
24 HOURS
FUNNY FARM
CAFETERIA
Fresh
MILK

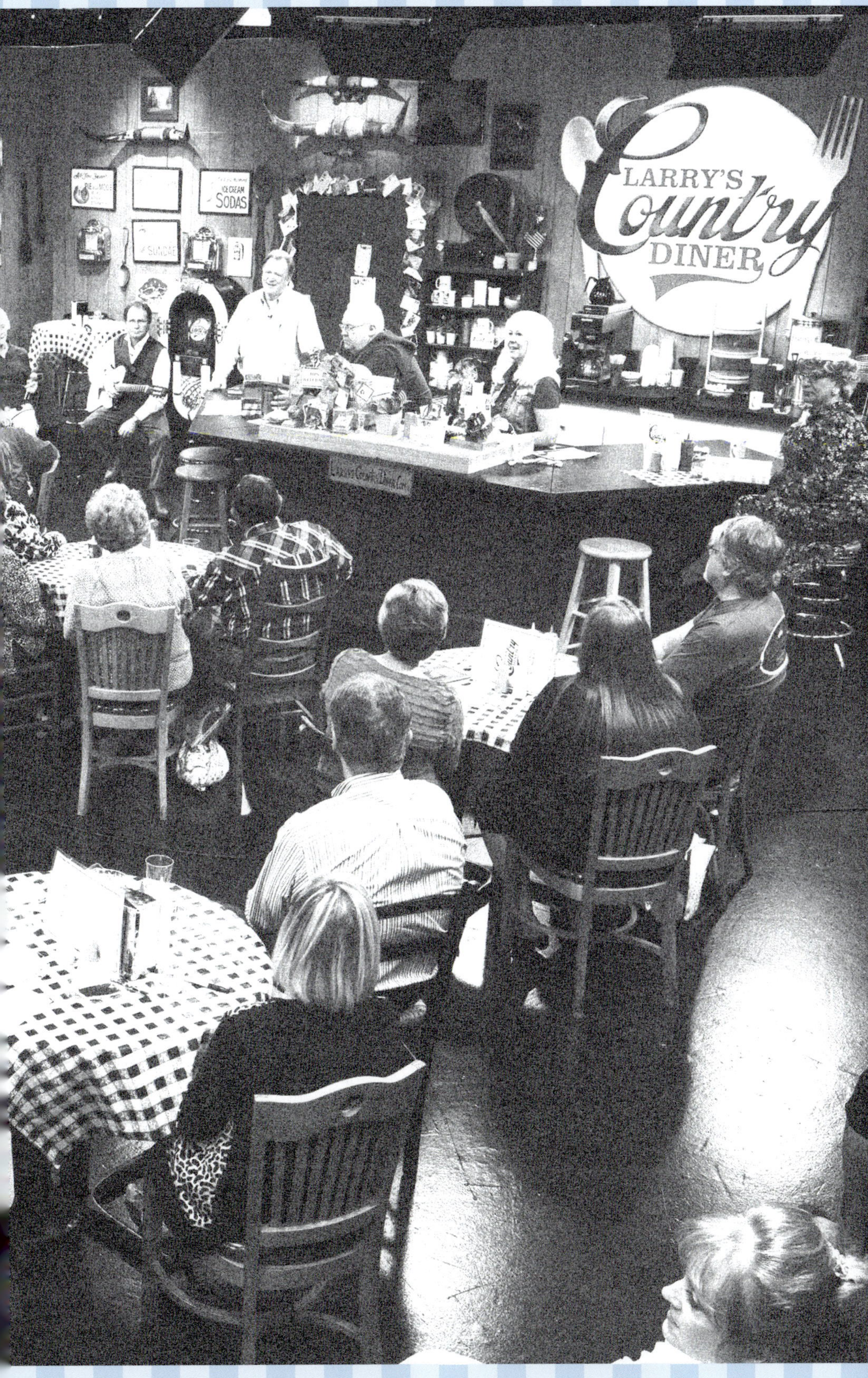

LARRY'S
Country
DINER
ICE CREAM
SODAS
SUNDAE

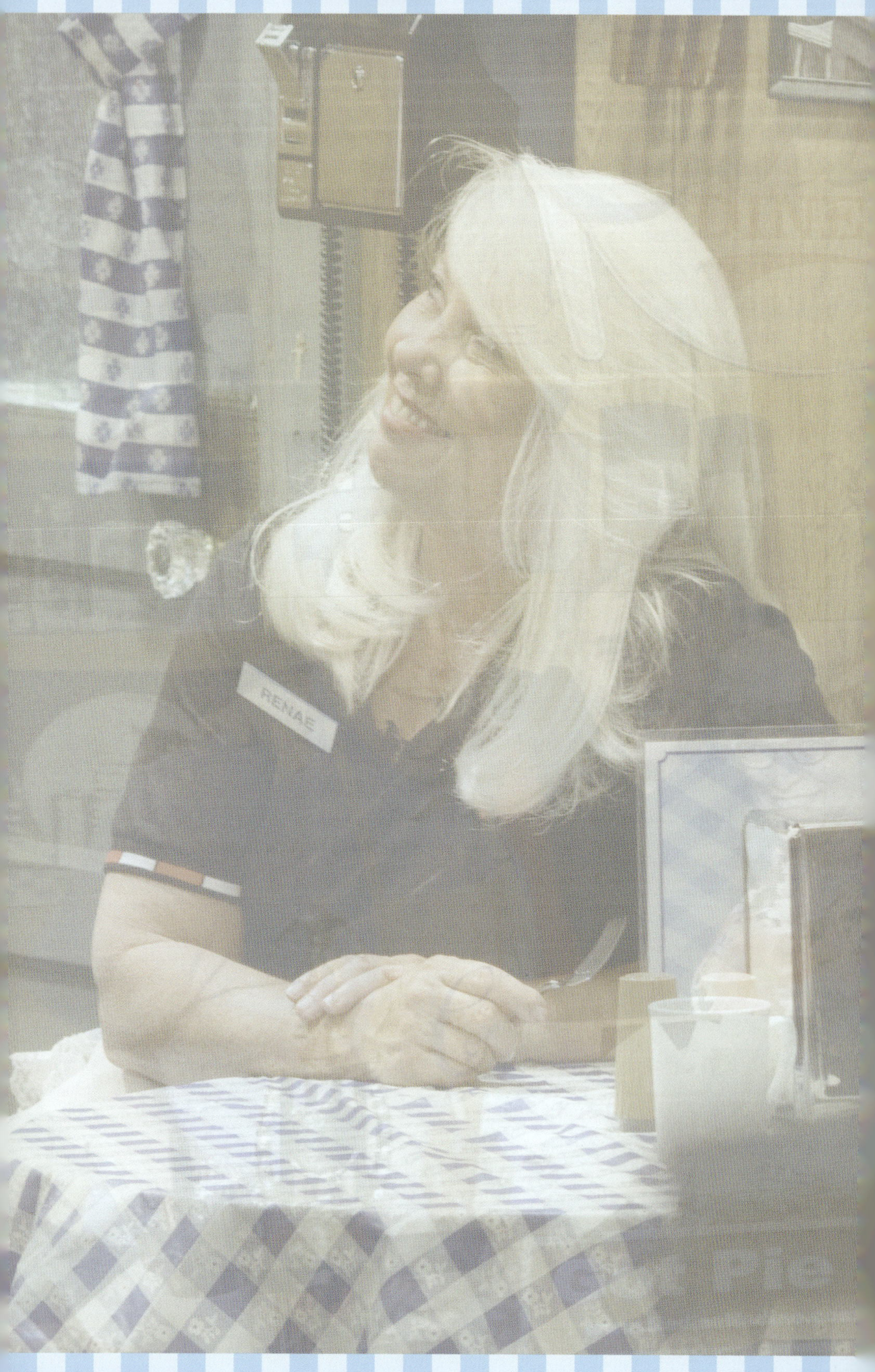
RENAE

During our first year we had a single artist hanging at the counter singing by him self. Then we started adding groups who had equipment to set up. Moving around the microphone stands, between the tables, around the counter and beside the artists started to get a little tricky...especially with cups of hot coffee or a tray of food. The funny thing is that I've had a few artists get so distracted with the deserts on my tray they actually ask for a piece of pie during the show.

I do have to say our customers at Larry's Diner are like no other. By allowing us into their homes every week they are a very important part of our lives and we become a very important part of their lives. I think that is what makes it so special when we finally get to meet. It feels like family getting together. We never take for granted how far folks travel to come see us at the Diner. And it's always fun when folks bring us goodies. Larry loves to show those special items on the show.

There are still a whole lot of folks that will never be able to make a trip to Nashville and experience coming to one of our diner tapings. So I would like to share a little of that experience with you.

The Diner Experience

After receiving a reservation confirmation from our office you would get directions and instructions on how to get past the guard shack on the day of taping. Since we tape 4 shows a day you will have a specific time to arrive There are signs that direct you to the side entrance of the building.

Once inside you will be directed to a holding room. Inside our holding room there are refreshments to munch on and chairs to wait. We have merchandise including our Country's Family Reunion video series and a lot of Larry's Country Diner merchandise to purchase.

Our holding room is much better than waiting in long lines. It's a place to gather and talk before you are seated in the actual DINER. It also gives early birds a place to wait without wondering the halls, which is not permitted. During this time inside the Diner we have artists doing a sound check, lighting being adjusted, tables and chairs being set and media arriving. It can be pretty hectic but mostly exciting and fun.

Nadine, Keith and I try our best to greet everyone in the HOLDING ROOM before folks are seated in the Diner. We give instructions, sign autographs and take photos, which allows more time after the show to meet and greet with the guests. Then when it is time ... you are led into the actual Diner studio.

RENAE

The Diner is already buzzing. You have to walk over camera cords and around cameras to find your table. When you enter you might see Randy or Paul from PFI sipping a cup of coffee or Ann Tarter getting her make up touched up. The lights are bright but it's still pretty chilly inside the studio. On each table is a place card with folks NAMES. Once everyone is seated the camera guys will let us know if we need to make any adjustments. I always tell everyone to find Gus from Springer Mountain Farms Chicken because he usually brings a guest. That guest is usually country music legend Jean Shepard or Jim Ed Brown. Behind the cameras we have a wall of bistro tables with stools. There you might find other artists that stop by just to watch the show.

If you are there for the first show of the day then you will hear Larry pray before we start. He always prays for the shows to go smoothly and everyone to have a safe and good day. He knows folks have traveled miles to get there and some have made sacrifices to be with us. Once he says "Amen" and "LET"S DO IT". The camera's roll.

During the show I serve everyone coffee, sweet tea, a meal and desert. And yes it is REAL FOOD and the best part ... it's FREE. The catch is that you don't get to order. Our pies usually consist of Pecan, Chocolate, Coconut Cream, and Lemon. I also occasionally serve a Chocolate Pudding with Whip Cream. So far we have had no complaints.

The only breaks we take in the show are for commercial breaks. At that time everyone's make up is checked and any technical adjustments are made. Then the tapes are rollin again. Once the show is over everyone remains seated while we make a quick promo with the artists. * Promos are recorded commercials that advertise the guests that are going to be on the show.

After the show is over we take about a 20-minute break. During this break folks at the Diner taping are able to take photos and autographs with the Guest artists and Diner cast. This concludes *The Diner Experience*.

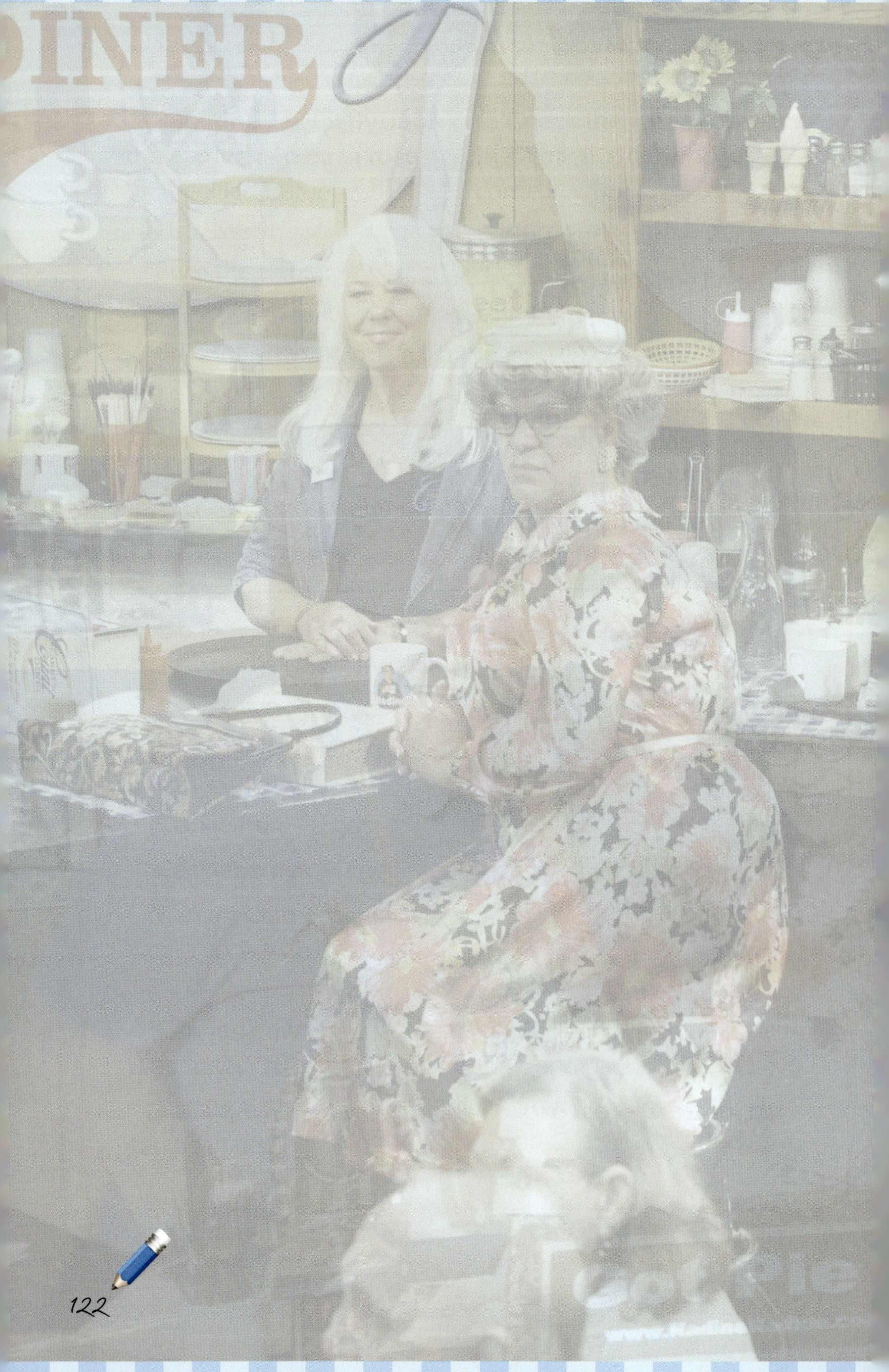
DINER

14

Diner Stories

The Door is Open

Let me set this up for you. The Diner set is inside a large studio or room. There are three walls supported by large boards. You have the back wall, which my work station is against and which features our big Larry's Country Diner sign and the swinging door. The two side walls make the set a room. The back of the set is open. Three large cameras are stationed there, so there is no wall. We have huge lights hanging from the ceiling and camera cables lying on the floor everywhere. A cute little guy whose name is Scott (whom we call Scotty so that we can say, "Beam us up, Scotty") runs around the counter with a camera on his shoulder.

We have tables with mismatched chairs and a hinged door that actually opens when Nadine walks in. The door goes "nowhere" except into the large studio that surrounds the set. As you can imagine, the Diner set can heat up pretty fast with the large overhead TV lighting, so we keep the Diner as cool as possible. We always remind folks coming to a taping to bring a jacket.

A few months ago, we had a fun group of visitors. Standard procedure is that guests wait in a holding room until we are ready for them to be seated on the set When they are seated, we still have a few minutes for sound check, so I walk around and talk to the folks, even move them around if necessary (just get everyone comfortable).

On this occasion, as I approached a sweet lady sitting at a table, I noticed she was all hunkered over with her arms wrapped around herself. When I got beside her, she looked up at me and said, "It's cold in here," and just as I was ready to respond, she pointed to Nadine's door and added, " Oh, no wonder. The door is open."

Gotta Get Teeth

A lot of folks have called and asked to come to our Diner tapings. One guy from Alabama called to see if he and his wife might get in. Sure enough, it looked like we had room. So he was going to check with Mama and call us right back. About 15 minutes later, the phone rang and caller ID revealed his name. But when the phone was lifted, all that could be heard was him yelling, "We can't come!" He was so distraught that I said, "Well, what happened? Why can't you come?" He said "Mama's got to

> "... I walk around and talk to the folks, even move them around if necessary ..."

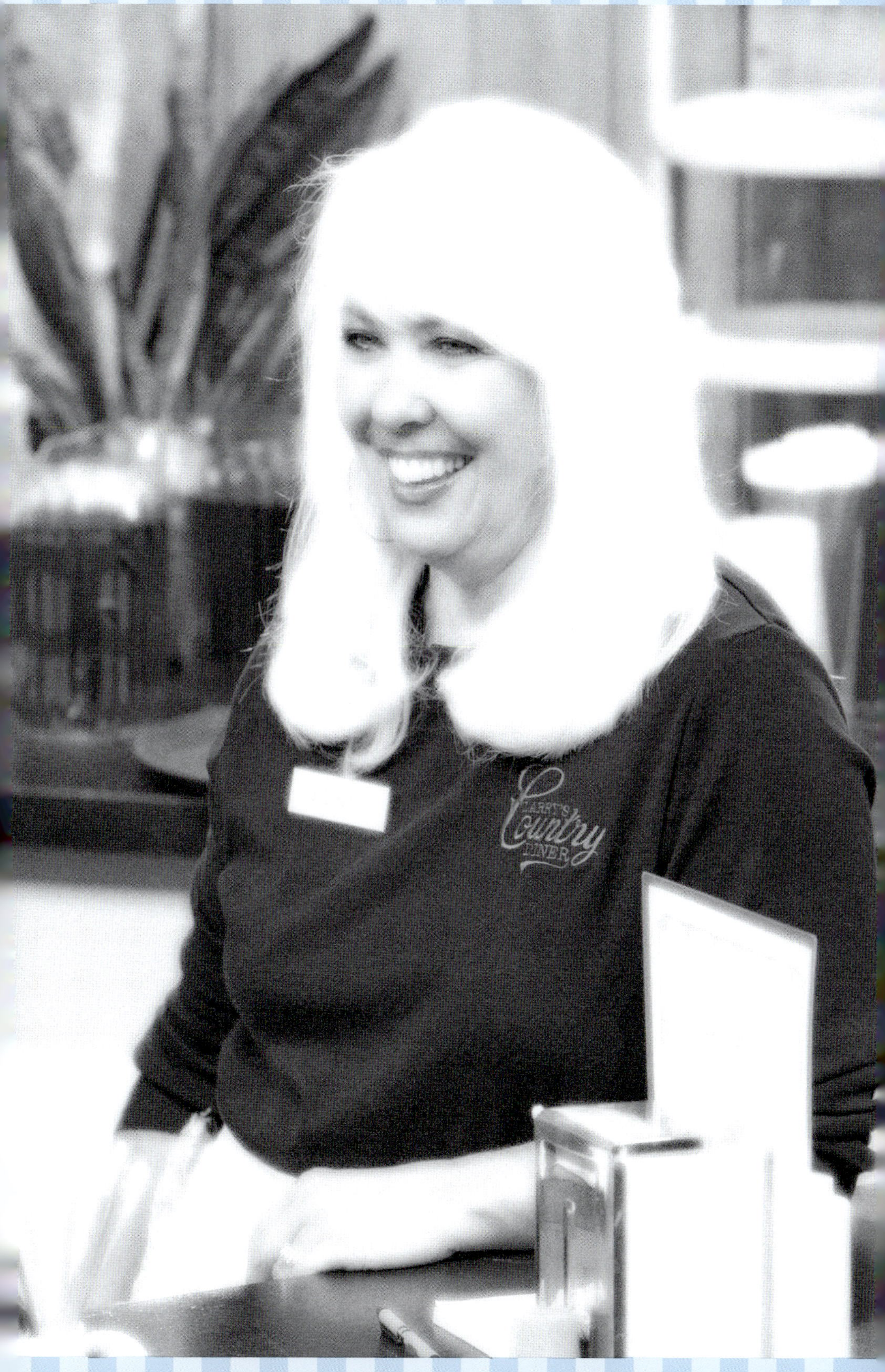
LARRY'S Country DINER

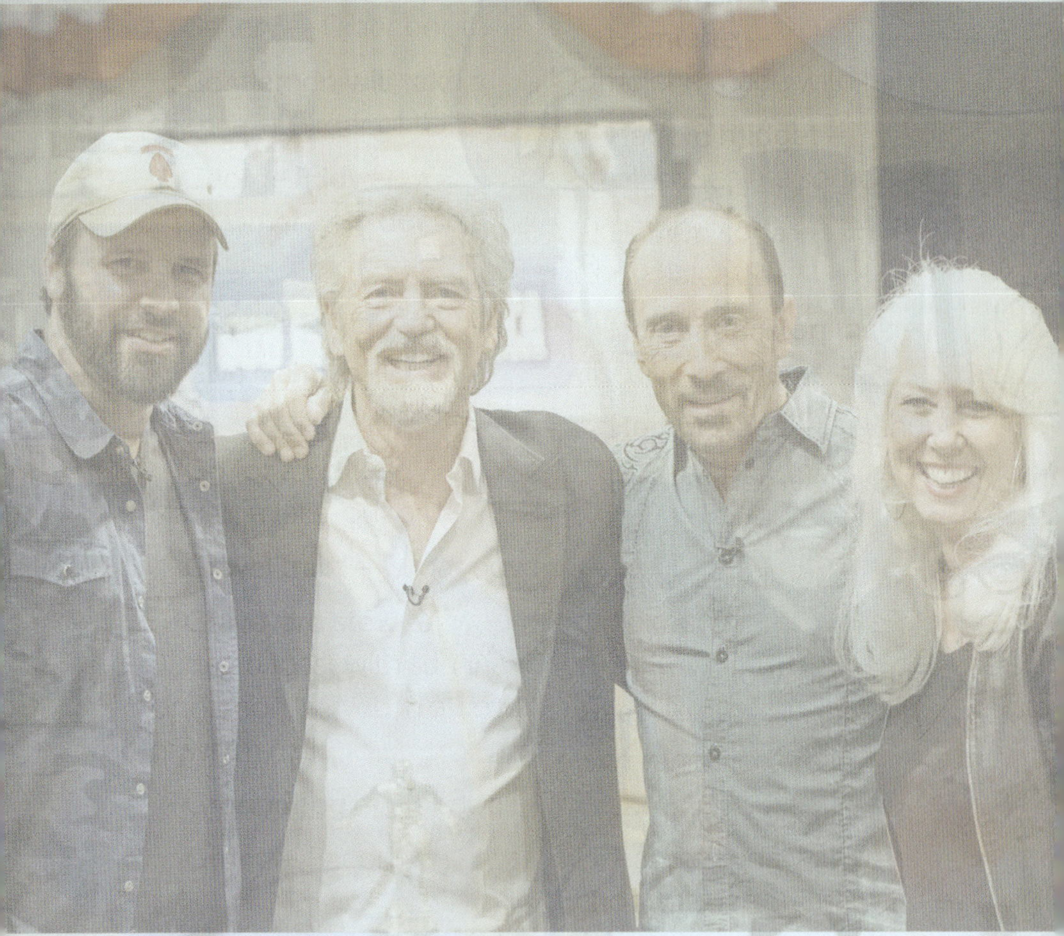

get some teeth. She won't come and be on TV unless she gets some teeth." I replied with a chuckle, "Well, go get Mama some teeth and come on." He said, " You think I can?" I said, "Sure. We will keep your name on the list." A few weeks later the phone rang and I saw who was calling. When I answered all I heard was, " Mama's got some teeth. We're coming."

Bad Waitress

After filming our first season of Larry's Country Diner and the show started airing on RFD TV, we received a call from a viewer. Most of the calls over the past eleven years had been about Country's Family Reunion, so when I was told it was in reference to Larry's Country Diner I was excited. Wow! This is great. A fan call. But the voice on the other end of the line was loud and angry. " Yes, this is Margaret from Little Rock, Arkansas, and I am never gonna watch Larry's Country Diner again." I was so surprised it took me a minute to respond, and before I could she added, "That waitress on that show does a terrible job! I AM a waitress and she looks like she doesn't know what she's doing. " My first thought was "Are you kidding me? I don't have any idea what I am doing and this is too funny!" But it wasn't funny to her. So I calmly said "Ahhhh, I am so sorry. This is Renae, the waitress from the show and I hope you don't stop watching because of me." I think I heard a gasp before I went on to explain, "You do know that I am not really a waitress, right? And that this is a TV show, filmed in a studio? Right?" Then, in a weak voice, she said, " Ahhh, no. I didn't know that. Well, you have a nice day now. I won't stop watching the show."

Of course I ran straight into Larry's office giggling. How exciting to think our viewers actually thought that Larry's Country Diner was a real diner and that I was a actual waitress--even if I a bad one!

Law Enforcement

Jimmy Capps our sheriff is a rather shy guy. He has always been in the background pickin' with the musicians either on a session or with the Opry Band. He's not one to call attention to himself. So when Larry gave him the local town Sheriff role he never dreamed he would get national recognition as a SHERIFF. To prove my point....

Larry's Country Diner has a lot of fans from Texas. Our down home diner southern hospitality and country music entertainment speaks to the heart of Texans. One couple arrived at our diner taping so excited. They had been on the wait list for quit awhile and to hear them tell it the highlight of their trip was to meet "Sheriff Jimmy Capps cause they were in law enforcement as well."

129

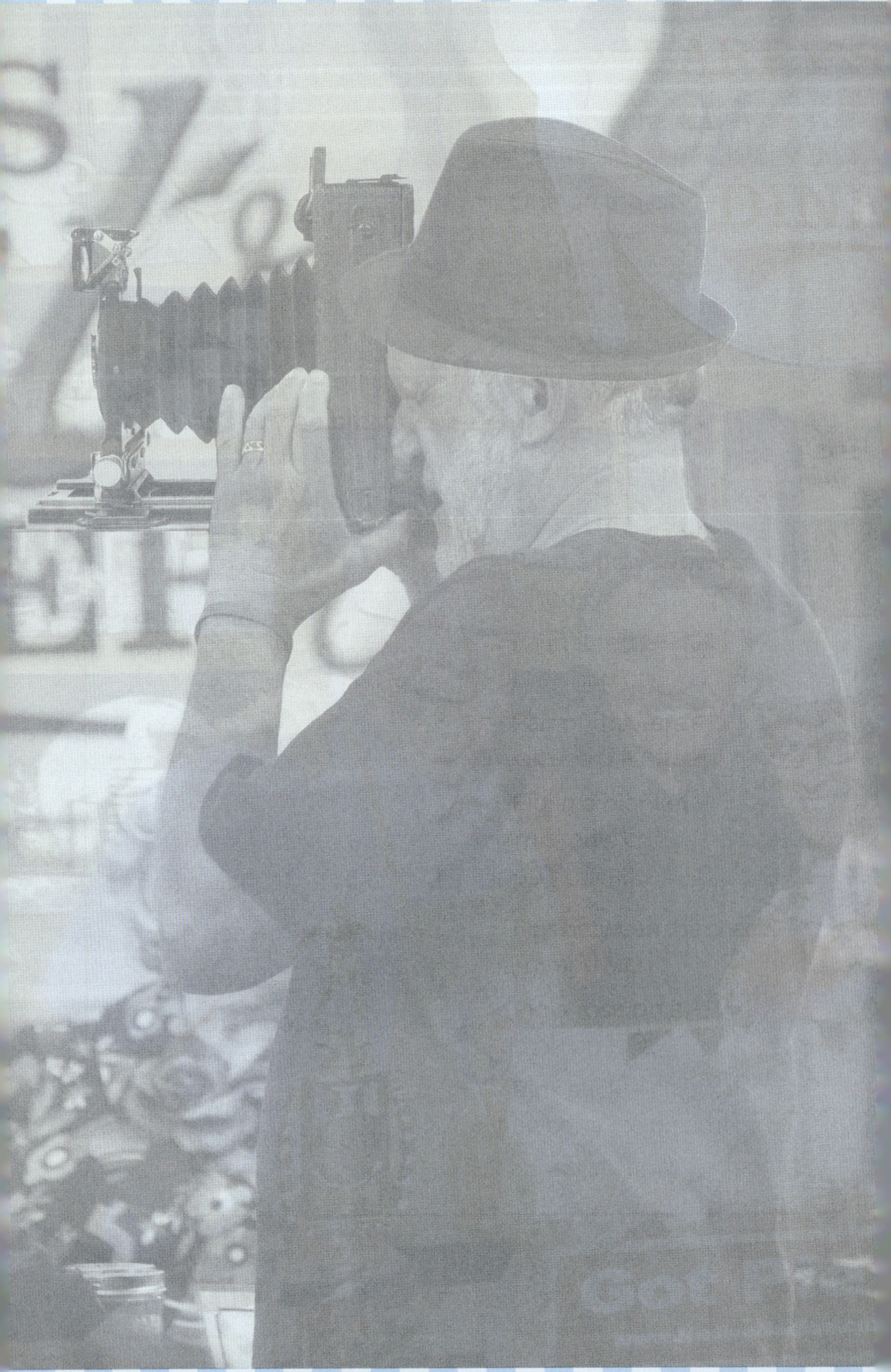

Paparazzi 101

The first thing I have to admit is that I don't take this "TV waitress" gig too seriously.

There are no real perks like the famous. I have to wait in line at the airport and at a restaurants to get a table. Let's not forget I actually have to WORK for a living. But once in a while I do get a taste of what fame may be like. It's like receiving a love note for the first time or a bouquet of flowers. And just like those special occasions I do not take them for granted.

Unlike the famous we are not followed around with flash bulbs in our faces or guys hiding in bushes, but we do have some press attend our Diner tapings requesting interviews which is nice. I feel very lucky and blessed when we have articles and photos printed about the Diner and cast. We have been in *Country Weekly Magazine*, *Lifestyle*, *The Tennessean*, *New York Times*, and *Branson News*.

Since we film quite a few of our own commercials in our office its usually just Larry and myself. And of course no script. We've taped cruise commercials, Starlite Theater commercials, product commercials and newspaper commercials to name a few.

So if you see me shopping or traveling through an airport and think it could be me yell ... "Renae the Waitress" I promise I will stop and chat.

16

In Case of Emergency

There are times when getting help can be very frustrating. Whether you need help with your shipment from Country's Family Reunion, booking one of our Cruises, getting tickets to our shows in Branson or trying to get Diner reservations there are some last – ditch strategies I will share with you.

1. When calling to get Diner reservations say you are related to Nadine.

2. If you need tickets to the Starlite Theater tell them Randy Little owes you a pair of boots.

3. If you are a country singer and want to be on the Diner call our office and ask for Terry Black.

4. Never place an order asking for "Jeannie" Shepard's book.

5. When calling to book our Cruise never try and save money by booking through a travel agent.

6. If you receive your order and it is wrong ... leave Jared a message that you are going to tell his Pop on him.

7. When you send a letter make sure you understand it will be read ... the good, the bad and the ugly ... and sign it.

8. If you are trying to reach us on the weekends ... No one is there.

9. To meet the Sheriff just yell "Hey Sheriff" during a live Grand Ole Opry performance.

10. If you call our office for help and Larry answers ... hang up!!

135

Guest Check

CHECK NO. 800529

See ya at the diner!